THE CITY OF RAVENS

THE CITY OF RAVENS

PARADOXES OF CONTEMPORARY INDIA

CARLOS VARONA NARVIÓN

Translated from the original Spanish by
Sonya Surabhi Gupta

PAPER MISSILE
NIYOGI BOOKS

Published by
NIYOGI BOOKS
Block D, Building No. 77,
Okhla Industrial Area, Phase-I,
New Delhi-110 020, INDIA
Tel: 91-11-26816301, 26818960
Email: niyogibooks@gmail.com
Website: www.niyogibooksindia.com

Editor: Keerti Ramachandra
Design: Shashi Bhushan Prasad
Cover design: Trisha De Niyogi

ISBN: 978-93-91125-46-2
Publication: 2022

Printed at: Niyogi Offset Pvt. Ltd., New Delhi, India

Contents

Paradoxes of India in the 21st Century

It lives between extremes, it embraces the extremes, rooted in the earth and drawn to an invisible beyond. On the one hand, a repetition of forms, a superimposition of concepts, a syncretism. On the other, the desire for totality and unity. And in its highest moments, the incarnation of a totality that is plenitude and emptiness, the transfiguration of the body into form that, without abandoning sensation and flesh, is spiritual.

***In Light of India* by Octavio Paz**

When will India find a middle point in anything? Will it ever achieve a balance between the thousand opposing forces that every day besiege it and tear it apart? How long before it sees a certain counterweight between its millenarian tradition and the 21st century, between the obscene excess of the new rich, and the misery of the vast majority?

These were the thoughts that kept crossing my mind during the first few days of my visit to New Delhi after ten long years. I had been to Calcutta and Bombay for various reasons in recent times, but not to the capital. In fact, I had begun to miss the hustle and bustle of Old Delhi and the tranquility of the new city with its British layout and wide avenues, that together constitute the capital of India.

On one of those days, I was caught in what seemed like an interminable traffic jam near Gol Market. It was an early February morning, fairly cold for New Delhi, and I had been in the car for quite a long time, with no heating. It was very uncomfortable sitting on the icy leather seat. When I asked my chauffeur to put on the heater he turned it up to the maximum, which made the inside of the car unbearably hot and stifling. When I complained that the temperature was too high he put it back to the minimum, that is, to zero. This happened over and over again. I couldn't understand why the man couldn't set the damn needle in the middle. He would twist the knob all the way from the right to the extreme left, then from left to right, much to my exasperation. I said to myself, Why can he not leave it in the intermediate zone, so we can avoid arguments and travel in comfort? But no! Obviously, these simple and practical suggestions did not find an echo in his mind. He continued to turn the knob endlessly with his left hand, from maximum to minimum. Tired finally of the absurd twisting of his hand, I leaned towards the dashboard of the car, and moved the needle myself, firmly and premeditatedly to the centre. With a certain degree of abruptness.

The gesture was unequivocal and authoritarian. Unusual for me! It was apparent from the expression of disapproval on the driver's face that he had not taken kindly to the abrupt end of his fiddling with the knob. He pointedly ignored my action and stared straight ahead thereafter. Evidently he was not convinced of the effectiveness of what I had done, even though we did manage a comfortable temperature. His attitude was beyond my comprehension. Perhaps he was thinking, these foreigners, they think they know everything!

From that seemingly insignificant incident of the car's heating I picked up some basic lessons and extracted many conclusions, in the following minutes itself. As I was a recent arrival in the city and still staying in a hotel, I had thought of buying some fruits for a light dinner or maybe to eat between meals. Yes, at last I was in India, a country famous for its many varieties of fruits like papayas, chikoos and of course mangoes. I had to take full advantage! How I loved mangoes! Even as a child, when mangoes were an exotic fruit and not easy to find in my country. Ignorant as I was, I did not realize that it was not the mango season! That would be a few months later, between April and August. Anyway, we had gone that morning to a fruit and vegetable market in Pahar Ganj, an area that in the seventies had been a popular hippy neighbourhood like no other. Even today it is a motley nest of shops of all kinds, where one can find everything from clothes to rice and spices, from imitation jewellery and books, to incense and leather goods, horoscope stones and small travel agencies.

I found myself with my feet resting on the ground, something not common in New Delhi since one always went by car from one place to another. I strolled among the little street stalls, finding to my amazement that all the vegetables, such as cabbages and cauliflowers, red cabbages and aubergines, and more, were miniatures compared to the ones we have in Spain and Europe.

Although I had had three short stays in India previously, in what one could classify as tourist visits, I realized that I had not noticed many things then which now became obvious very early on. Like the tiny size of the vegetables. This was to happen to me repeatedly in the early days, to my surprise! It once more demonstrated the sidereal distance between a mere visit, and actually living in a place. I wondered how it was possible—how in such an immense country, with a land so fertile and ancient, between the Himalayas in the north and the tropics of the south, with their palm groves and forests with huge trees, such tiny fruits were produced. Tomatoes were like eggs, and lemons, without any exaggeration, little more than large olives! With a few exceptions, in all the stalls I found that the vegetables, even potatoes, garlic and onions, seemed "abridged" by a capricious bonsai reduction. How was it possible? Only carrots and watermelons seemed to have been saved! And those fruits, like oranges and apples that were of a standard size, were imported!

India had always meant for me, the finding of that mid-point between the extreme options that life offers, however difficult it may be. It was the Middle Way that Buddhism had advocated. That, along with analyzing suffering and the means to avoid it, was among the greatest contributions to humanity. But that was something I could not see anywhere at that point of time. Maybe, things are not so easy! That ideal of the middle path, between asceticism and desire, between illusion and reality, between the material and the spiritual… It was not a given already there, but something that could be achieved only after a journey of search. It was a journey I was prepared to undertake!

But right now, I found everything astronomically away from the Buddhist ideal of the golden middle path, or *aurea mediocritas* mentioned by Horace. Aristotle, the teacher of Alexander who came here, would call *aureas mediocritas* the golden mean. Two centuries before that, according to legend, Buddha had had an interesting experience. The Enlightened One, the Great Awakened One, had wandered through many places before achieving that state, deepening an endless path of extreme asceticism and renunciation that seemed to have no bottom. It was the complete opposite of the twenty long years when he had enjoyed the life of a prince, with all sorts of pleasures and comforts. Now he was in the opposite phase, but his pilgrimage from place to place, from teacher to teacher, was fruitless. He did not seem to find peace. One day, it is said, when he entered a village, he heard a musician tuning a veena, a beautiful stringed instrument halfway between the lute and the sitar. And suddenly, there it was! In front of him! That which was so precious, which he had not found in his long march. By tuning of the strings to the correct and balanced middle point without being overly tense or lax, the strings vibrated with beautiful music. That was the key! The inner tuning against extreme tendencies in which the ego, the I, becomes entangled and does not know how to get out of it.

It is a universal rule that you must avoid extremes if you want to achieve health, emotional and mental stability on a personal level and peace and growth in the social sphere. Yes! The midpoint is certainly most difficult to achieve and it is not about mediocrity, rather it is about excellence, about balance!

The biggest challenge for India today is to avoid social extremes, to build majorities with a dignified and hopeful way of life.

According to the innumerable statistical data available, we learn that in ten years, the middle class in India grew from 300 to 500 million. If statistics are to be believed, I would like to say that the opening up of the economy in the 1990s was a success, and that the speed with which the recovery of the people's wellbeing was effected, has been impressive. However, the parameters used in the measurement are problematic. According to some studies, those earning $5 a day are said to belong to the middle class. This sounds ridiculous when compared to say a near-by country like China, where even in rural areas the salary is twice this in many cases. It is true that the country's figures under various heads have marked an astronomical growth in recent years, especially in large cities, but practically half of the population is excluded from all social attention, as in social welfare schemes. And it is possible that it will be so for generations to come. More than 500 million inhabitants do not yet have access to electricity, or suffer frequent power cuts. Recently, the Director, Institute for Water, Environment and Health of the United Nations, described this situation as "a tragic irony", that such a large number of citizens have mobile phones, but "do not have access to a basic necessity related to human dignity such as a toilet." This is a shortcoming the country cannot afford. If large sections of the population, rural and peasant, still do not have access to modern education and health care, India cannot project herself as an emerging reality, a nation on the move. Yes, it is hoped that everything will scale new heights and change in the coming years! But until then?

It is evident and natural, I suppose, that after centuries of hardship and deprivation, there is in India a great desire to arrive running, even with the tongue hanging out, to a superior situation. However, the figures are obstinate and overwhelming. According to data available to me from March 2017, India has 1,170,178,305 mobile phones. In contrast to this, only about 400 million people (35 per cent of the population) have access to adequate sanitary facilities. There is a lot of talk about new technologies and the internet, but two-thirds of the population does not have a connection. Despite India being in sheer numbers, the second largest internet market in the world, faulty lines are constant, the equipment obsolete, and until a few years back (2016) 65 per cent had no or limited access to the network. India still has only 84 television sets per thousand people (USA has 938), and 8 personal computers for every thousand citizens (against, Australia, with 565).

Ironically, in spite of such shortages and widespread poverty, as reported by *The Times of India* (1/19/2016), the country has the fourth largest population of millionaires (with incomes of at least one million dollars) in the Asia-Pacific region. Heading this happy list is Japan, with 1,260,000 people. According to this report, it is expected that by 2025, India will experience a 105 per cent growth in the population of millionaires, that is almost half a million: 483,800. It seems that the emergence of the new rich is much faster than that of the middle class which is comparatively slower. The principles of moderation, balance, the "middle way", linked to the Buddhist goal of attaining peace of mind, seem to be far from this India of the 21st century. It is now defined by "cool" gurus who play golf and receive politicians and actors in their ashrams.

The old socialist system of Nehru and Gandhi weighs like a millstone around the neck and has little to do with this 21st century of computers and globalization. The salaries of officers in the government sectors are comparatively rather low and every Indian wishes to become an entrepreneur, however small, or go abroad. Yes! It is the only way to have a healthy income, they believe.

After Independence an institutional secularism was fostered, parallel to a long and complicated democratic process, governed by the separation of powers. From this great clash of cultures that ended with Independence and Partition, at least something has remained in India of the best of Europe: democracy and the aforementioned separation of powers. The stated ideal being the common good, the functioning of justice, despite high levels of corruption, is vital for the creation and foundation of the middle classes. In the long run, these elements constitute the most positive achievement from the long contact with the British, even though a mixture of admiration and hatred has defined their relationship over several centuries.

One cannot deny the truth that many are the paradoxes, impossible of resolution, in all fields. Extremes of excess or of lack, find a fertile ground both in history and in the myths of India. The clearest and most obvious case is that of the god Shiva. He forms part of the Indian Trinity (Trimurti). His name means "the auspicious one", the one who brings good omen, the beneficial and the alluring one. He, the great god, appears before whoever approaches him, as a perfect synthesis of the old prehistoric, Dravidian India: the lord of the beasts and forests, with the later Sanskrit and Hindu deity of the great cities and temples. Through the mythology, Shiva sometimes reminds one of Janus, after whom January the first month of the year is named. He like Janus is the god of beginnings and duality and time, whose double face looks to the past and the future.

The paradoxes of Shiva, in effect, incarnate destruction and creation, for which the disappearance of the old, of the exhausted, is necessary so the new and the rejuvenated can take its place. And nothing expresses this better than Shiva Nataraja! Yes, here in India, I always had Shiva in mind, he being the Lord of Change, the eternal dancer who renews the world, who destroys it and recreates it almost instantly, with each movement and the next. Yes, sudden and unforeseen changes, like the one that had just occurred to me, had much to do with him. Besides, we were at the beginning of the year!

Lord of Death, but also of life and birth, Shiva is the Hindu deity par excellence, of transit, who looks towards extremes. In the

Mahabharata he is depicted as having three eyes, the third being the one with which he destroys desire (Kama), which tries strongly to tempt him and end his prolonged asceticism. Soon, the gods, unable to endure such a prolonged abstinence, manage to soften him so that he rekindles desire from the ashes he had consigned it to, in order that life may continue. To which he finally accedes.

Among the hundred or even a thousand names of Shiva, according to *Linga Purana*, and ten thousand according to *Mahanyasa*, he appears in mythology as the great Lord of the Gods, Maheshvara, the creator of the primordial sound OM, Omkara. He is indeed Mahabaleshwar, the immovable Lord, the immutable one, although he is also present, without there being any contradiction in it, as Nataraja, the perpetual dancer, who with his dance constantly recreates and transforms the cosmos. Among his almost infinite titles is Guheshvar, lord of the deep caves, although he is also known as Kedar, and as Girisha, being in both cases the sovereign of the summits. The deep and the elevated are not contradictory for him! The summit and the abyss constitute his very nature. He is, at the same time, the one who terrifies Bhishma, and the one who infuses serenity, Aghora. In the same manner that he is Maithuneshvar, the lord of intercourse, of endless sex even though he is Gambhiresh, the ascetic, the austere renunciate of lust. Likewise, he is known in this sense as Apamnidhi, the lord of the seminal fluids, even though he is also Kamanashe, the relentless destroyer of desire, and especially Yogesh, the lord of yoga and restraint. In one of his best known epithets, as the propitious, the benevolent, he is Shankar, but he is also Bhairava, the destroyer, the annihilator. Thus, Shiva is the head of the household, Grihapati, owner of the home, and at the same time he is Bhikshatan, the beggar. This immeasurable deity is Tamasopati, the lord of inertia, of passivity, while also of fire, and lava, Pavaka, besides being wind and storm, Marutta. He is all that and also the ever beautiful, Nityasundara. At the same time, he is the terrible, Rudra, and the annihilator, Sarvatapana. And he is the Supreme Reality, which transcends the apparent opposites.

Attempting to decipher these legends and epithets at the beginning of the 21st century with our Aristotelian and western rationality, governed as they both are by the principle of non-contradiction, is something that makes the most asserted certainties falter and seems to put everything into question. At a deeper layer of their meaning, we are not told that opposites are exact contraries at an identical point and place, but that Reality itself may have different manifestations and angles, which, although apparently "contradictory" to the senses, does not ultimately turn out to be so in transcendent consciousness. It is not an empty game of words! For at a higher plane, both opposites bend to touch each other, establishing a flow between them, intense as a ray. Seen from an integrative perspective, closer to the heart than to the mind, they are not exactly the affirmation and categorical denial of the same, but rather something which somehow complements each other. Intuition, not reason, in a cyclical dynamics, even in such different presentations, binds them and makes them interdependent as a natural continuity, such as the valley and the summit. Something like the burn caused by ice, "the opposites are reconciled without destroying." Only thus can you be the lord of desire and renunciation. He is! He dances, and with him the whole cosmos does, achieving the infinite weight of its matter, it yet has the lightness of a swirl of his dance.

All this, that is, my presence in India, with this complex and fascinating culture on my mind almost twenty-four hours a day, had begun in the most fortuitous way just over two months ago in Spain, more specifically in Barcelona.

Although a native of Madrid, where many of my vital references are to be found, and where my wife lives, I had been in Barcelona since a year for professional reasons, and it was already beginning to fatigue me, although I alternated between Madrid and Barcelona on weekends. By a quirk of fate, absolutely everything would change so rapidly, giving an unexpected turn to my life that I could hardly believe it, let alone assimilate it.

This is how it transpired. At the beginning of December 2013, I was invited to a wedding at this coastal Spanish city by an Indian friend with whom I had worked years ago on a building construction. I don't usually go to weddings. I could count on the fingers of one hand the number of times I have been to them. I carry no special memory of any of them. On this occasion, however, a special set of circumstances had come together combining my life-long attraction for India, and a period of inactivity, almost paralysis, which made me accept the generous invitation immediately. The preparations for the betrothal was really impressive! For weeks now, the event had been the subject of extensive speculation and gossip in Barcelona. Since the event could not be less than the best, they selected unique locations for the marriage-related festivities such as the Maritime Museum and the National Museum of Art of Catalonia (MNAC), locations which had never been used for this purpose. It was a happy circumstance and a win-win situation for everybody, although there was some criticism of such extravagance in times of a national economic crisis. Naturally the one in charge of organizing the events, a specialist in dealing with high-end, uber exclusive clients, was required to maintain, as a part of the contract, maximum confidentiality about his clients hailing from the distant Orient.

I arrived at the place, at dusk, and noticed among the guests who had come not only from India but from the most diverse places in the world, the senior-most representatives of the Catalan government, the Mayor of Barcelona, and several foreign dignitaries. After all, it was the wedding of the niece of the Indian steel magnate Lakshmi Mittal! Just as I reached there, the bridegroom, a 36 year-old bank executive, rode past me on a horse and entered the garden leading to the area where most of the guests awaited him, beside the grand staircase. As per tradition, he trotted under a floral arch, with many people surrounding him. The horse, of course, was immaculately white, the same colour as the groom's traditional outfit, which made the fuchsia of his turban stand out. These two colours, fuchsia and white were unofficially taboo for the guests since they were the colours of the bride and groom's attire. Although the guests had been discreetly informed about this, it did not prevent many turning up in just those colours! One could see clearly a mix of traditional colourful Indian dresses mainly worn by the elderly, the parents of the bride and the groom and close family, as also some younger members of several European families.

Bedecked in diamonds and heavy gold jewellery, the bride entered the museum under a large vermilion canopy, surrounded by the bridesmaids carrying open trays laden with red roses. At night, after the wedding ceremony, the bride and groom, along with the guests, enjoyed a pyrotechnic spectacle accompanied by Montjuïc's fountains in full splendour. It does not happen except on very special occasions. A wedding gift from the Barcelona City Council to the couple! To match the high standards!

One of the guests who had travelled from Mumbai to the great Mediterranean city on a specially chartered plane, was Mr Mukesh Sharma, a famous businessman, who lived between London and New Delhi. His business, as in the case of a large number of Indian tycoons, ranged from software to construction, to the sale and marketing of the most varied international goods. At the cocktails before dinner, the person who had invited me introduced me to him as a landscape architect, a domain in which I have made my career. He looked at me intently, then said that he would like to talk to me. After a few moments, interrupted by the betrothal program, he told me that he had recently bought a piece of land in the Indian capital where he planned to build his new family home. In a conversation lasting barely a quarter of an hour, we had closed an appointment for the next morning in my study, though it was a Saturday, since on Sunday he was to return to New Delhi. He said he wanted to know "as soon as possible" about some of my projects for private homes.

With a fine moustache, and perhaps slightly dyed brown hair, Mr Sharma possessed elegant and relaxed manners, typical of one who is accustomed to giving orders, of one who never waits for anyone, rather whose demeanour demands that people wait for him. He spoke English with a slight nasal tone and a clipped accent which I would later find is common to that class of Indian men enriched by huge profits from real estate and a buoyant infrastructural equipment and development business.

"You should see the place where I bought the land. It is in one of the best and biggest areas—Chanakyapuri, a diplomatic enclave near Rashtrapati Bhavan, the residence of the President of India, and formerly the palace of the Viceroy," he said with great self-assurance. He declared that he liked the area, as it was away from the crowds, but not too far from the farm houses of Chattarpur and Vasant Kunj.

"I hope the work would be of interest to you," he added not wasting a minute.

"Of course!" I said enthusiastically, driven by an intense desire for a change of life and place.

"I trust you! I will await you then!" he said tersely, extending with both his hands, in the respectful Indian way.

What was said was done! As seldom happens. The distinguished Indian with elegant gestures arrived in a taxi early the next morning directly from his hotel, to the office cum workshop from where I was temporarily operating. With great speed, summarizing my ideas, given that we had little time, I showed him folders and magazines which featured most of my projects covering many years of experience. Some of them had not been carried out for various reasons, but I did show him two residences that had been completed in the environs of Madrid.

Considering how reserved Indians usually are in terms of their opinions and expressions, I was somewhat disconcerted by that elegant wedding guest, showing interest in me, in my work—more than potential customers in Europe, usually do. From the start of the conversation that morning, which would change the next years of my life, he seemed determined that I start to work immediately for him. It meant going to New Delhi as soon as possible, to see the land and begin work on the project. He certainly had in his favour the fact that I wanted a change of environment and place, notwithstanding the fact that I liked the city of Delhi itself.

The offer and the terms were excellent. Mr Sharma was one of those people who did not think things twice, and never hesitated. Because of his work, the volume and number of operations in many different fields, he was accustomed to deciding everything, even the most important, on the go. Sometimes things work out better intuitively, not by presentations and long discussions. He liked my approach, and the three or four main ideas I presented as starting points when conceiving a private house. It surprised me, because we did not know each other at all, nor did he know, through other people, of my work.

It had been just about two months since my first meeting with Mr Sharma, with Christmas in between, which seemed to me enough time for preparation. The time I needed to close and conclude all pending matters, which were not many. I had reached a kind of stalemate in my life and in my career, a period I usually call a time of "plugging holes". But that was now a thing of the past. It already seemed so far away! I was going to dedicate the present, once I settled down, and saw the land and its surroundings, to formulate ideas, write notes, outline projects, experiment with different materials, and sketch the images that came to my mind for that particular residence in New Delhi. It had been decided that my wife would come after about two months, and help me with the actual process of settling down.

On the long flight from Madrid, via Munich, I concentrated on the master lines of the house that I was supposed to design and build within a time frame, yet to be decided. Of course, the signing of the work contract was still pending, though I thought it a minor matter, given my strong faith in the owner. Not only had he sent me the airline ticket in preferential class, and a hotel reservation for the first week, he was also a well-known and reputed businessman with offices in various parts of the world.

I took advantage of this unending journey through the clouds to make a multitude of sketches, and mentally turn around various alternatives for walls and roofs that I believed could take shape on a land I had not yet seen. This entailed building the house with open spaces and large, well-connected rooms, without corridors, with very high ceilings, in cubic and linear volumes, without a single curve or column! It was very important that it possessed a certain energetic autonomy, with good use of sun and natural heat, not only with photoelectric solar cells, and natural heating of water, but also to have light in all the rooms.

To inspire myself, at the time of offering contextualized alternatives to the massive work that I was dealing with, I informed myself, well before leaving Spain, of traditional Indian knowledge on construction, *vastu vidya*, the science of inhabiting—*vastu*, which means abode and *vidya* which is a science. This ancient wisdom, about which I only had certain basic concepts in the beginning, is the sacred knowledge used in the construction of temples, which for centuries, had remained partly hidden. This knowledge was rooted in the Vedas, almost four thousand years ago, and its objective was to re-balance the scope of the "inside" and the "outside" of a structure, between the microcosm of inhabited space, and the immeasurably larger macrocosm: the earth, the air, the space, and the universe itself. This exchange of energies between the intimate and the exposed, through walls, stones and other materials, restores, for well-being and meditation, the circularity of energy between the elements and the human body. It is a game between stability and mutation, between the changes of light due to proximity or distance, from the sun and the moon.

From this point of view, the lines and planes when building something, act as a yantra, as a scheme of orientations and cosmic energies, a *vastu purusha mandala*, in which man interrelates intimately, both with the nearby cosmos, the water, and the winds, as with the distant one, the planets and the stars. Harmony with the environment, in the Indian tradition is based on principles similar to Feng Shui. It is the art of attracting health and prosperity to the home, through forms and architectural elements. The structure of the universe, summarized in numbers, in geometric schemes, orients the construction of the house or the temple. Electromagnetic fields, the attraction of shapes and masses, orientation, proportions—all these ingredients, whether they are known or not, directly affect the human being, and one must know how to apply them as per the key they hold while arranging the house and the use given to each space, thus distributing the fundamental forces of the universe.

Quite away from these concerns, Indian architecture almost in its entirety today has adopted the tastes of the oil-rich, typical to the Arab Gulf, Qatar, or Kuwait, with a not inconsiderable mixture of the Russian oligarch. One would say that the battle has been lost, if it ever was initiated, to preserve some Indian construction characteristics, both of structure and "adornment". Very few modern buildings in this country try solutions based on the knowledge of its rich past—which is not that far back! Which is still present everywhere, in front of one's eyes! It is not as if there was a model that may not be repeated, or was there no model at all. They had it! They are therefore not justified in making meaningless banalities, without an origin in something solid, something their very own. In short, a brutal price has been paid for moving from the 20th to the 21st century!

As soon as I arrived in New Delhi, I wanted to visit the site at dawn, and in the twilight, with all the lights and forces at work. I had in mind some characters from India who had always held my attention, the sadhus and rishis, sages from this ancient land with special powers. As a result of their deep meditations, they knew how the visible sinks its roots in the invisible, in the spirit, in that which is beyond senses, colours, forms, or sounds that can be perceived. Much like this non-rational perception, I wanted to choose from among the various possibilities of construction.

Mr Sharma had told me in the very first meeting, to my big relief, that he did not like the big villas of the new rich located in the southern parts of the city close to the airport, like Gurgaon, the new satellite city—rootless, an enemy of the pedestrian, and which could as well be located in an African desert, in Canada, or Australia.

He preferred Chanakyapuri, he said, a "classic" neighbourhood, in a quiet, tree-lined area. Considering the fact that there were no vacant plots available in the Golf Links, or Sundar Nagar neighbourhood, and he wanted a certain proximity to the airport because of his almost continuous travel, he had chosen Chanakyapuri. It must have cost him a real fortune, given the price of real estate there.

After knowing his wishes and needs, the first phase involved the process of explaining to him the conception of the house and the general lines of its development, with multiple options. Once I had them clear, I would execute all of it on the plans and the model. He wanted it to be a very contemporary structure yet rooted in the Indian tradition, using local materials, like marble and sandstone, but with some Spanish elements, such as glazing.

Like those of his class, who do not suffer hardships and firmly believe in devotion to Lakshmi, the goddess of wealth, Mr Sharma told me about his vision of India with an unmistakeable elitist outlook. Despite possessing a certain natural elegance, self-criticism had not even touched him and he saw the half-full bottle only in his own favour. On the other hand, although totally wedded in his way of life to modernity, rationality, and modern business practices, he told me that he went to the temple from time to time with his wife, and on several occasions I saw an orange dot on his forehead. From facts that came up in the conversation, it was clear that he hailed from an old family that had made its money at least one generation ago, from the sale of land. His paternal grandfather had been in the Congress Party almost from the time of its inception. And yet he was very clear that his residence should be in the diplomatic neighbourhood near Raisina Hill, where the power of the British Raj had resided for a short time.

On several occasions, I was about to ask him why rich and privileged people like him did not contribute, through establishing foundations and trusts to finance projects for the growth and improvement of the nation, but I did not really get down to asking him this, because I thought more opportune moments would come, once I had established greater trust between us. But no! Such an opportunity never came! Maybe because I did not have much faith in the answer! Sometime later I would learn that in addition to local and foreign NGOs and Christian missions, there are some foundations in India dedicated to the help of disadvantaged groups and communities, and to the development of specific areas, even if they are just drops of light in a great ocean of darkness.

Since India became independent, there have been at least two Indias—the India of Nehru, who said that "dams are the temples of modern India", and the India of Gandhi, who wanted to create a future in his own way, of a virtuous, traditional, and intensely spiritualized India. That vision has been left in a dry dock, permanently stranded. It is buried under the rubble of poverty and failed developmentalism, in the dashed hopes of improvement in the lives of many of the 1.39 million people.

Through a close friend of his, a real estate mogul, Mr Sharma had found for me one of the best architecture studios in the commercial centre of the city, where I could carry out my work with maximum comfort. Luckily it was next to the beautiful and strange park of Jantar Mantar, right in front of the hotel where I had stayed for two intense weeks soon after I arrived. I took advantage of the proximity to go for late afternoon walks there, in the bustling surroundings of Connaught Place and the curious garden of the astronomical observatory. I bought various things in the nearby Tibetan and Gujarati Market, from papier-maché Kashmir boxes to small bronze figurines.

The studio itself was spacious, bright, and in principle met all my requirements so that I could deploy my labour effectively during the long days of work. The first phase would be dedicated to the design of the house, with the support of two draftsmen and a design engineer. The second phase would be the construction of the building itself, sufficiently representative of its wealthy owner, without giving the impression of megalomania, or pretentiousness as was evident in the residences of many Indian businessmen. To develop this, I had the support of two surveyors, and a small team of craftsmen, who would work in tandem with the workers on site.

However, my arrival at the place where I was to start my assignment, in the first week of February, was not quite encouraging. The reason basically was that from the very beginning I felt an absence of cooperation in the studio, especially from the management team. Perhaps because of some strange and incomprehensible jealousy, arising from the suspicion that I enjoyed privileged treatment from the "powerful"! Or maybe it was simply due to the manner in which I had presented myself, and installed myself instantly at one of the design tables. Mind you, I had not taken anyone's place nor had I caused any displacement! But that was probably what had happened. They saw me as an interloper, a strange creature, "fallen" from the skies, for whose convenience a huge sum had been paid to acquire this studio. And that too for someone who did not even know English! Unforgivable in this environment. It was a mixture of perceptions, in which my Mediterranean background weighed heavily against the Anglo-Saxon one that prevails here. Add to that the mantra that made it abundantly clear that each one must solve his own problems. Whatever it is, the truth was that everything was so unfriendly and cold! The people in my team were impersonal, if not positively hostile, each individual focused on his own task, rather than those of the team. There was little mutual trust and respect between us. I felt certain that the deliberately imposed distance was unnecessary, and the clear apathy and disaffection in the treatment, was something I was not accustomed to.

Anyway, the studio was certainly big, both in space and personnel, with more than twenty technicians and other operators, most of them young architects in practice, adding up to about fifty people in all. They seemed to have been recruited from all over India: Gujarat, Uttar Pradesh, Orissa, Bihar and Rajasthan. The management team consisted of four main architects from Maharashtra and Punjab. One was the executive director, the other three in charge of basic areas. As for the rest, it was like in a traditional workshop, almost medieval, in the good and bad sense. It was the typical relationship of the official with the apprentice, everything being done with few drawings and preliminary preparations. The direct and artisanal stage of the realization prevails with models in some cases. A practice observed throughout India

So, each day of my stay reaffirmed my impression that the atmosphere was very cold towards me. It made me feel like I was in Toronto, Manchester, or Sidney, not in India, not in a country with a warm climate, with vibrant colours and tantalizing aromas, and easy communication with the surroundings as well as each other. How different is the Mediterranean character! My French and Italian training, made me observe the huge difference that prevails in this region, perhaps the result of the Anglo-Saxon influence in the big cities.

And yet when they interacted with each other and other colleagues jokes were exchanged and light hearted banter was normal even among the management team itself. I never got along with the management team, by the way! No one made the slightest effort to include me in their conversations nor did I try to participate, except in the beginning. Our interaction remained at the level of a basic courtesy. It would have been interesting to be able to share points of view, different architectural and work experiences, or simple formulations useful for both parties. But it was not to be. It seemed as if nothing could be done to change that, at least in my case.

This is something I had noticed from the beginning. It is difficult to work as a team in India if "team" is understood as a living organism, as an engine in which each part fulfils its mission, but also serves as a transmission chain for all others.

Something that I found very difficult to adapt to right from the beginning, was the use of British imperial measures in the country perhaps for the sake of continuity. The measurement of an average plot of land, such as a garden, is universally mentioned in yards, an interior space is measured in square feet. With objects, the measurement is in inches. There is hardly a mention of metres or centimetres, which disconcerted me continuously. To this one could add the constant use of acronyms to refer to any institution, university, corporation or centre. If you do not master that alphabet soup, you"re out of the game!

On one of the first afternoons I was there, while I was returning to my hotel my attention was drawn to an incredibly large flock of crows that populated the sky. The sky was full of wings and sharp black bodies gliding, with a flow that did not seem to contradict their very high number. It was as if a black cloud was taking different forms.

From my hotel room I could see them concentrate on the Jantar Mantar Park, the 18th century astronomical observatory, built by Jai Singh II. It is similar to the one he built in Jaipur, a city that bears his name. I had always been struck, during my earlier visits to New Delhi, by this place as it stands between antiquity and the future, with an ethereal, utopian aspect conferred by the strange constructions carried out to calculate planetary movements and configurations of the Sun and the Moon.

They hovered over these strange geometric structures, the stairs that led to emptiness—on those concentric walls that seem to concentrate cosmic forces that escape our understanding. Though they were ordinary crows, of an intense jet black, silhouetted against a polluted white sky they looked like eagles. It was a spectacular sight! I had never seen such a large gathering of birds like those! Yes, I had observed similar scattered flocks of swallows and other small birds, but nothing of these dimensions. It was almost scary, even though crows are not really aggressive at all. Later in the evening, the sky, veined by the copper of the setting sun, which was not visible, was spectacular! It seemed totally unreal, that strange brilliant sky of a dirty red, furrowed with black birds!

Although I always liked to travel, even if it was for work-related reasons, I could not live for long periods in hotels…three weeks, a month… That was the limit of my endurance. Thus it was crucial for me to find a place to rent as soon as possible. Although it would have been more comfortable, cheap and quick to find an apartment, I did not want to feel encapsulated, no matter how spacious. I had to choose between being in a house with a small garden in the colonies of New Delhi, which in principle did not satisfy me fully, and the attractive possibility of renting what is generically known as a farm house on the outskirts of the city. Interestingly, despite the country name, nothing is grown or produced in these properties that emerged in Chhatarpur and Vasant Kunj, beyong Mehrauli, in the southern part of New Delhi, at the end of the 1970s. These are coveted places of escape and recreation for the upper class families in the capital. It is also common in some other Indian cities to have a large and luxurious "pied à terre." The idea is not to live in them, but to dedicate them to social events such as weddings and weekend parties.

It was a curious and instructive experience to visit them with real estate agents, known locally as brokers, and meet some of the owners. In fact, I met up there with the intermediary who had been recommended to me in the Spanish Embassy, and together, we made several appointments with others specialized in the famous farm houses. We started on Church Road, in a neighbourhood called Park Lane, and in the following days we moved towards the east, towards the southern end of Chhatarpur. Each house, both inside and outside, represented a different world in its design, and in the layout of the garden. Some tried to imitate a rustic and earthy style, others were pretentious; some even aspired to ape a somewhat kitschy Versaillesque style. Almost all of them, especially the most recent ones, shared straight lines, large windows, and a tendency towards the luxurious and nouveau riche minimalism, popular in the Emirates and countries in the Arabian Gulf.

Many of the houses were most impressive with the expanse of lawns, extensive gardens, and numerous trees, and the spaciousness of their living quarters. I was struck, however, by the early aging of construction materials, and in general by their roughness and poor finish, despite the good quality stones or wood used. Some of these properties were true palaces, hidden from view by high-walled fences. I learnt in a short time, however that no matter how attractive some were, they were impractical for a foreigner who wants to live there for a limited period, and who does not have an army of caretakers and gardeners, and all supervised only by a trusted manager. And yet, though it was against all logic for me to take such a big place, and against the advice I had been given in the studio, not to go so far, I was determined to get one of those magnificent residences. I thought that even if I had to spend much of the day in the horrendous traffic as I commuted between home, office and construction site, at least on weekends I would be a happy man! Those gardens with large palm trees, the open spaces inside, far from the great pollution of the city, were idyllic, therefore enormously tempting. In addition, the temperature was several degrees lower because of the tree mass, for which one would be grateful during the better part of the year.

In reality, it turned out to be far from what I expected, due to a long list of inconveniences. Worst of all it was the time wasted when caught in the terrible traffic jams, given the enormous distance to the studio, in Connaught Place, the centre of New Delhi. But as I still did not know this, or did not want to acknowledge it, after a few days of looking for a property that best suited my needs and desires and the limit imposed on me by my new job, I rushed to sign the contract with the owner of this particular house. So strong was my urge to leave the hotel, to be in my own space, that I moved into the house the very day I signed the papers.

The place in which I live has always been very important for me, even when in transit, even if only for one day. Not for nothing had I become an architect! For me, a house is like a second skin. In it, I have all the books and objects that had drawn my attention and I had gone on to accumulate over time. At last I was there! But problems began to appear on that very day! The first was the deception in the purchase of oil for the power generator by those who took care of the property. This was immediately followed by several serious inconveniences in the house and the colony. In the almost complete month that I was there, I spent a good part of my time repairing damages, which the owner ought to have taken care of before letting it out, and investing in interior lighting…in the end, for nothing!

The decision to give up the house, however attractive and spacious it had appeared, was taken after a month during which many things happened that impelled me towards it. Of the six bathrooms distributed over both floors, not one could be said to not have serious problems, such as poor or no water supply, issues with electrical connections, and faulty faucets... As for the kitchen, by itself much larger than the ones in many European apartments, was unfinished. Even though I demanded it every day from the owner, it remained unfinished! Likewise, the bedrooms, quite large and regular, almost square, as I like them to be, inexplicably had no blinds, and there were no curtains either. It would require tens and tens of meters of fabric for so many bare windows. To add to the myriad other problems, there was the impossibility of dialogue with the housekeepers who supposedly were in charge of the maintenance—two young boys who lived in a makeshift dwelling under the master bedroom. They did not speak a word of English nor did they show any sign of wanting to be even slightly friendly. They had been living there for months, perhaps years, taking care of the house, and now a foreigner had descended on them. It did not matter that he was going to feed them in the near future.

But beyond these "material" and practical difficulties, in this complex stage of my installation in New Delhi, the worst was that on the very first night I spent in the farm house there were all kinds of sounds emanating from somewhere that made me uneasy. They kept increasing and became more and more annoying as the hours passed. The strange thing was that in the two visits I had made to the farm house before renting it, I had not encountered them, or maybe they did not exist in those moments. There was a big house opposite mine, totally silent during the day, apparently with no one inside, but on whose roof the servants descended after sundown, organizing a chaotic nightclub. All attempts I made later to end that unpleasant surprise that assaulted me every night were useless, because the owners lived far away, and there was no one who was bothered to be responsible for anything. The other louder and most persistent of all the noises came from the nearby airport. Every three or four minutes you could hear the thunderous landings of aircraft. The approach line seemed to be right there, above the house! Of course I was fully aware that most of the international flights to Europe and Asia and the Middle East, land and take off from the Indira Gandhi International Airport around midnight.

But that was not all! Scattered in that apparently tranquil area, were several open spaces meant for weddings, and other varied events, which, almost every day from dusk until well into the early hours of the morning, played Bollywood type music, unbearably strong and crushing. And to think how beautiful and refined Indian classical music is! How could these Bollywood rhythms be so obnoxious? Especially when you listen to them per force. It is real agony, like being put on a cross. Was this, I asked myself, the sign of two irreconcilable Indias, which I would witness throughout my stay there?

No doubt I had not been there at all hours to see how the place would be during the day and the night. A major failure on my part! But who checks and verifies everything! In this situation, from the third or fourth night I started taking pills to help me sleep. And when the effect wore off in barely two hours, it was still there, the agonizing music and the assaulted ear drums, thanks to the planes. They were the only ones who seemed to be eternal!

As always in India, the wooden windows, which did not fit well, were neither insulated for the weather, nor sound proof. Thus, the nights became long, immeasurably long. I had left the city, looking for silence, repose…I needed to rest! I needed calm to put my mind and my work in order. Instead I found many more sounds! How was it possible?

A major, or should I say the biggest disadvantage of living in this house was outside of it. I had not taken into account the difficulty of living so far away from the centre. It involved an unbearable waste of precious time day after day, plus the fatigue of travel. My mind, my body, were not as before. They had become much more fragile, much weaker. Distant and unattainable seemed the weekends that I had dreamed of spending at home, in the garden…

Also, living so far away meant that I could not rest even for a little while after lunch, something that not only my stomach would be grateful for, my brain and my general mood too. When the days are so long because of travel and the work itself, at least for me it becomes important to divide the day, with a pause at noon, for a couple of hours. More than a majestic sleep, which except in midsummer seems excessive, in order to be well I need what in Spanish is called a "cabezada", a nap, to refresh the mind, to be more relaxed and creative—something which one would suppose is the engine of my work! Yes, a certain disconnect of just twenty minutes, parallel to digestion, half an hour at most, is truly invaluable.

All these elements formed a bitter cocktail that in my inner dialogue, I drank throughout the day. The noises, the unrest, the early dawn, made me feel really miserable. The stay in India that had caused so much excitement, for which I had been waiting for years, was becoming a nightmare, I thought. It was the first time in my life that I experienced the strange state of which until then I only knew the name: Insomnia! To that fateful cascade of events was added the fact that it was already the end of March, and an intense heat had begun, which forced me to sleep with air conditioning. And there arose a new problem that deepened the insomnia! I was not used to that loud, persistent, enormously disturbing hum.

During those weeks, I avidly read everything that fell into my hands about insomnia, advice and observations that clearly distinguished between temporary insomnia caused by stress, as was clearly my case, and the chronic condition. That was easy to understand! However, the sword of Damocles always hangs by a thread when the worst is feared: Persistent lack of sleep could turn chronic. Yes! The bad thing was the fear that gripped me, that the temporary would become permanent! Worse was that my work began to suffer from the exasperating situation. The exciting start of the initial days in solving the project's main lines, calibrating the terrain and its surroundings, in testing the selected materials, was somewhat slowed down, if not paralyzed. Although with his usual discretion and elegance Mr Sharma said nothing, there is no doubt he noticed my distress during our periodic meetings.

I tiptoed around like a zombie those days, under various natural drugs, such as valerian root, or hops—all of them very light, as I could see on a few nights when they barely had a numbing effect on me. Not to say no effect! Thereafter I tried discreetly some Ayurvedic remedies. I visited several centres in the area known as Green Park. And yes, a full body and head massage with hot oils relaxed me and made me sleepy during the day, but when night came, the same battle raged: not enough relaxation to carry me on the wings of slumber, to sleep, as other mortals did! That was my modest desire! Only a self-administered anxiolytic achieved the sublime goal of putting me to sleep, but for a maximum of two hours, maybe three at the most.

I kept repeating to myself at night that anxiety and restlessness are precisely the motors of creativity. But the fear of not being able to sleep did not abate! In the first few weeks of moving to the farm house I was in a mess—a heart-breaking feeling between my attraction for India and the joy of actually being there, and the predicament I found myself in. It was a kind of daily destruction, and daily resurrection. Was it perhaps a great test that India was putting me through? Maybe! Experience shows that worthy things rarely occur quickly and easily. The problem arises when the pitfalls are unpredictable, like night navigation without maps, and few instruments. Clearly, it wasn't going to be possible to just get there and enjoy. There had to be something in between! Something that would touch me to the root of my being!

I also tried doing moderate physical exercise throughout the day. Music was an invaluable help. Sometimes I would sleep with the earphones fixed firmly in the ears to reduce the sound of planes landing, or the howling of dogs, which seasoned the total lack of silence. I would choose very special pieces of jazz, classical and sacred music, or sometimes, contemporary composers, like Arvo Pärt, or John Taverner, and his impressive "Lament for Jerusalem". Laments and ecstasy would become the same simultaneously, in my ears. That wonderful music comforted me from the anguish of sleepless nights.

The intense stress brought on by insomnia had repercussions on my breathing and the rhythm of the heart. A kind of emotional short circuit! In those days I kept sending constant messages to my wife, night and day. She acted like an authentic Ariadne, until I got out of the labyrinth that I had got myself into. It was she finally who convinced me that I should give up the house, no matter if I lost the deposit of several months" rent, as per the contract. She came to help me soon, first with making the decision to leave that place, and then to decide on another house. This time, one in Sundar Nagar.

I wanted to believe that all those difficulties that kept knocking at my door, from the most prosaic, like opening a simple bank account, to the most subtle ones, like a deep feeling of loneliness, of isolation in that new environment, meant a process of intense learning, the step prior to a serious test. Such a test would make me accede to another plane of perception, of existence. In short, of a relationship with myself and with others. I wanted to reconfirm once again, that crises do not happen in a fortuitous way, but always precede a certain lesson to be learnt and never forgotten. Yes! Nothing that happens is random or accidental, but comes from something. It is the consequence of everything that happened before. And it is also for something! It points us to a direction that we must know how to see and then direct our steps towards it!

The key that opens all the locks is in the mind itself. It lies in the need to detach oneself from the closest, most pressing problems, it consists in finding the centre of all actions and knowing how to remain in it, becoming a witness of acute sight, beyond the ego, beyond our little biographical self.

Fortunately, when I was down and despairing, and low on energy, that house at the outskirts consuming all my resources and hours of sleep, a colleague gave me good advice. From the other side of the line, many miles away, he told me briefly: Do as in chess, take a retreat!. Indeed, this matter of the house had got out of hand and I had to make a decision immediately. Yes! I had to act as in a chess move! Without delay, I had to take a firm step back. Yes! And I"d take it now! I had to make a clear withdrawal from the matter, from what I perceived as an attack. Of course, it was not personal in this case, it was an attack not only directed, premeditatedly directed at me, but at someone who had to show a defence, backed up in a whole strategy, so that it did not eat me. With its attacks and retreats, with its absolute simplification of two sides identified by colour: black and white, the truth is that the chessboard represents a symbol of life itself. It is something primordial, a mythical combat, but at the same time governed by well-known and well-defined rules. It was therefore, in itself, also a paradox. With the brute strength of every attack, of every struggle for survival, a subtle short-and long-term strategy had to be woven. On such a board chance, or unexpected luck, counts little, and it is each player who chooses from the almost infinite possibilities of the moves, which in turn lead to instant inevitable consequences.

Yes, chess is a reflection of the world and life, framed undoubtedly in a schematic binary dualism, but perhaps for that very reason, a real and operative one. As with almost everything we have encountered since our birth, it has these two doors, alternately closed and open. And there is no doubt that its origin lies in India! From the 8th century onwards, abundant literature was written about the tactics and strategy of chess. And from there, on the journey to the West, via Iran and the Arab world, where, among other historical crossings, the expression "checkmate" (from Persian *shah*, king, and Arabic *mat*, dead), concluding in the Middle Ages in Europe as a finished product. Since ancient times, *chaturanga* was played here, on a board without squares, of 8 x 8 sections (as the 64 of chess), called *ashtapada*. That's where the devas and asuras, gods and demons fought for power over mortals on the board of the world.

Surely, this diagram of eight squares multiplied by as many more, displays an intense symbolism in the number '64', present in fields such as archaeology, and in various games, as a metaphor of the infinite, of the unlimited quadrants of the universe. Transferred to daily games, played by four human hands, it is summarized in winning, knowing full well that existence is an immeasurable game, without a definitive end. Sometimes the game continues, even after death, until everything, the truth and the hidden details of someone or something, are revealed, justice thus reaching a final balance. Darkness and light are intertwined in it, and complement each other in complex ways. One, white would not exist without the other, black! One of the two begins but may not conclude with the victory, although it may be the same one. It is the site of primal battles, with all the imaginable chicanery. It is sublimated brute force, something that is achieved with calm dialogue on a board, although all passions are still in play. Existence is sometimes summarized in this binary movement, which represents the duty to choose at a given moment between entry or exit, left or right, down or up. As in a miniature painting, all the feelings and passions of existence are there, concretized and summarized. It represents a micro encyclopedia, which in its boxes and strategies contains all possible power struggles, jealousy and doubt, loss, fear, and courage, but above all the instinct for survival.

I had never been particularly passionate about chess, but when I meditated on the advice, it made complete sense! This apparent game is a step from the vagueness of chance to the precision of the will! From the non-manifest to the manifested, from the hidden to the obvious. On a broader plane, the opponent is not a person, but destiny. The confrontation and the concrete fight takes place between two sets of sixteen pieces: eight pawns and four executing couples: two towers, two horses, two bishops, a queen and a king. The pawns are something like the light troop, which is located in the front line to repel the attacks. And after them come the heavy components of the army, with towers/chariots, and combat elephants/bishops. On another level, and contemplating all of this with a superior perspective, there are the king and queen in their protected, and above all, leading place. This may be just one more game, although it brings together like none other, the human adventure encrypted in advances and setbacks, in partial gains, in euphoria, or discouragement, until the ultimate conclusion of gain or loss.

Sundar Nagar is a colony of the forties and fifties, developed by a hundred odd wealthy Indian families, shortly after Independence. There were three such colonies that stood out in New Delhi. At the eastern end of the British urbanization, distinctive for their tranquillity, and the excellent quality of construction, they were Golf Links, Jor Bagh, and Sundar Nagar. The house I took on rent was of two floors, next to the boundary walls of the zoo, and a short distance from the great fortress, Purana Qila. On the ground floor with a garden, lived the landlady, a retired doctor of advanced age. From the first floor, with a wide glazed veranda, I could see the arboreal mass of the gardens on the sides and the zoo in front. Roars of tigers and lions were heard from time to time, and from there, peacocks often came to the roof.

The worst thing for me in New Delhi was the traffic and the deafening noise of the trains and heavy vehicles on the network of the huge arterial roads. The sound was a continuous bellow that did not subside, as in other places, with the night, but rather like the breathing of a living being, stretched over the whole twenty-four hours. That discomfort, rather nightmare, always showed its worst and most terrible face when I had to go somewhere relatively far from home or the studio. During the early days of my stay, when I had to attend a dinner, or go to some place related to work, the addresses often seemed to me riddles and enigmas. Puzzles that had to be solved on the march, an endless march. Extension II, Block G, Sector III, Number 23-B. A number that, by the way, was rarely followed by 24, or preceded by 22, B seldom following A, or coming before C. On the other hand, the most capricious cuts and continuations occur in the most unexpected places, which forces truly detective searches until one locates the required address. It always made me wonder, if it is so difficult to find a place in spite of having a local driver who knew the city well and spoke Hindi, how would a foreigner at the wheel, who does not know the streets or the language, manage? It seems that a genius had devised this devilish numbering system to take revenge for something or to extend a curse indefinitely. How much time is wasted looking for places! How many thousands of hours throughout the year are spent in traffic jams and journeys! How easy it would be to give the streets names and identifiable and consecutive numbers! Unlike in many other places in the world, only the great avenues of New Delhi, such as Janpath, Prithviraj, or Akbar Road, have recognizable names and numbers.

Fortunately, the route from the Connaught Place area where the architect studio was, to the Chanakyapuri site where the house was to be built, was usually clear. It skirted the compounds of the major embassies: USA, France, China, Canada, among others, with delays only at the starting point, which was near Jantar Mantar, the most popular and official site to hold all kinds of protests. Almost every day of the year there were demonstrations—by unions, social sectors, ethnic minorities, farmers expropriated for almost nothing, poorly paid teachers, Dalits claiming job quotas, Jats and others. Everyone finds their natural protesting space there!

Like it or not, the city where you live always ends up becoming a second body. It is an invisible body that, although it cannot be seen with naked eyes, is somewhere in a nebulous place between our memory and our bones. It ends up being like an organ, like a hand, or a foot, that we always live with, a second skin that covers us and we take for granted, when we go wherever we go. Not in vain, living in this or that city, are we under its particular influence throughout the day, over its telluric currents which, whether we want it or not, constantly penetrate us. And they do so with the irradiation of their accumulated history, their milestones and idiosyncrasies, and with the suffering and happiness of the many generations of their inhabitants, even though we do not know them. Would I be pleased with it or not in the future, I don't know, but with the step I had taken that Saturday in December, I had committed myself in Barcelona to the project of a great house for Mr Sharma. And for that I would have to be in New Delhi for a period of not less than three years, which is what it would take to finalize the design, obtain permits, and then start the construction once the final plans were accepted. Then the ground had to be prepared for the landscaping and gardens, which along with the actual construction, would take at least two years. By the time the internal fittings and fixtures were put in place it would be at least six months more. The project as a whole would stretch over three years. Though finally it became four!

Yes! Despite all the difficulties, New Delhi was already my city, and it would continue to be so for a long time! It was hard to measure the proportion of the things I liked to the ones I disliked about it. One of the most annoying features, for anyone coming from the West, and also causes consternation even to the locals who have lived outside, is the impossibility of walking. It is because of the absence of viable sidewalks and places to walk, except for parks like the Lodi Gardens, one of the most pleasant in the city. I started walking there in the mornings before going to the studio. The driver used to drop me by the entrance of the stone bridge, and twenty minutes later he would pick me up, at the roundabout of the Amrita Shergill Road. In that little but well spent time, I briskly crossed the circular rose garden and passed by the tombs of the Lodi dynasty, enjoying in those early hours the dew in the grass, the multitude of birds and the wind in the branches of the trees. Even in the summer I walked there, amazed by the flocks of kites and the crows bathing in the water that flooded the lawns.

Outside of these and other privileged green areas, numerous in the city, though badly maintained, the breaks on the sidewalks, the kerbs half a meter high, the most varied and unexpected obstacles, such as walls, booths, improvised parking and others, make walking just impossible.

As against these immense and endless spaces, there are the tiny shops of Khan Market, a ghetto of foreigners and of the nouveau riche, a favourite haunt. Although it was not one of my preferred shopping centres it is nevertheless one of the few places where you can find quality products. There is an intense paradox here, a most accurate image of what India is! The apparent absurdity of having huge grounds and large empty buildings, in a huge city, while its stores, pharmacies, self-service stores, bookstores, and shopping places ail from not only being really small, but even microscopic at times. In the best-stocked book store of the city, Bahrisons, in Khan Market, it will hardly be possible for one to move, not only to search for titles but even to open a book and read a few lines. You will be systematically pushed, or at best asked every two or three seconds to step aside for someone to pass or get at something behind you. The same will happen in the small shops and fruit and vegetable stalls of Bengali Market or the INA. They stock the best products in the city, no doubt, but it is almost impossible to enter! The only explanation that seems plausible is the exorbitant price of the land. Something that can only be explained by supply and demand in a city of nearly 25 million people.

It fills me with dread to think that all the major cities of the globe could be in the near future like the current Asian capitals Hong Kong, Manila and others—megapolis of endless traffic jams, where people walk like zombies, talking to their phones without worrying about what happens around them. The problems that affect most of them are similar, although of course, there are at least two widely separated levels—the rich and pristine on one hand, such as Tokyo and Singapore, which suffer from lack of personal space, and those which clearly suffer from overcrowding, lack of sanitation, poor transportation, as in India—Kolkata, Mumbai, or New Delhi. The problems afflicting them are similar—chaotic wiring, very scarce treatment of garbage, and acute lack of water—not to mention the extremely high cost of housing. As many other cities, Shahjahanabad and the antecedents of Delhi were located along its river, the Yamuna, from where they took the water for their daily life. Today this is not possible because sewers and chemical industries release their effluents into it, plus a general careless attitude of dumping garbage into it, has transformed the river into a drain.

Among its many problems of shortages and structural deficiencies, water is one of the most serious in New Delhi. Along a network of 10,000 km of pipelines, almost 40 per cent of the flow is lost through leakage. And only a tiny part of it is filtered! Though the government recently invested Rs 1,300 crores on its improvement, it managed to cover little more than half the treatment of waste water. Many measures are needed to improve the existing equipment and piping so as to prevent losses. But what is also entirely necessary is cooperation from industries and citizens to stop or avoid pollution of rivers and aquifers.

At present, there are about 30 megalopolises on the planet, cities with more than 10 million inhabitants, a dozen of them with more than 20 million: Shanghai, Canton, Seoul, Mexico City, Cairo, Sao Paulo and more. New Delhi this massive city-state, city-region, today stands at 25 million inhabitants. Two out of every five inhabitants, even from the best areas of the city, are suffering from serious health problems, lung, liver or genetic, because of pollution. Where will this endless escalation which threatens to turn the planet into a giant conglomerate of concrete and asphalt, end?

The reasons for migrating to the big city are known. People seem to identify progress and opportunities with the agglomerations, although sometimes the final result is the opposite. At least in the western sphere, New York was the first overpopulated city. In the 50s, it already had more than ten million inhabitants. Except for cases such as Mexico City or Sao Paulo, the unbridled growth of megacities throughout the 20th century and the beginning of the 21st century moved towards Asia: Tokyo, Shanghai, New Delhi, Beijing, Hong Kong, Manila and others. Urbanization of the planet is, perhaps, inevitable! However if we act in time, with a general awareness, which seems unlikely, its negative effects can be reduced and even reversed.

It is true that since the change of economic direction in 1991, by Prime Minister Narasimha Rao, and his finance minister, Manmohan Singh, the per capita income has trebled to the present level. Even so, many million Indians subsist on a dollar a day, or even less, which means living well below the poverty line. Despite the peculiar populist socialism initiated by Nehru and Gandhi which eventually disappeared, so many class differences persist, and brutal and obscene social inequalities exist side by side, separated only by a few metres. Liberalization, and changes driven by globalization, notwithstanding, Indian economy remains very protectionist. There are still no foreign supermarket chains or others like them because of an understandable apprehension that they would ruin traditional Indian business.

Because of the accumulation of household garbage for whatever reasons, greater dangers exist. For example, the extensive use of highly toxic elements such as mercury, lead, cadmium, and chromium not just spread through the atmosphere as intense poisons, they are absorbed by the soil, contaminating groundwater. Indiscriminate and unscientific disposal of electronic devices like computers, mobile phones, etc, allows hydrochloric acid to be discharged into the atmosphere, causing severe respiratory illnesses. Mercury on computer screens, for example, is extremely toxic, and after inhalation or ingestion causes irreparable damage to the brain, as well as to the eyes and kidneys. The same happens with the cadmium of the boards, batteries and inks, which affect the bones and the nervous system. Children and young people are the ones who are most vulnerable, and they are the most exposed.

Perhaps the only thing that to a certain extent equates the rich and the poor in India, because it is a shared experience, is the terrible loss of time in getting from one place to another. The difficulty and unpredictability of reaching places, whether in a luxury car or a modest rickshaw or bus, is common to both. Yes! The real problem in this country is commuting. It is the one big deterrent to going anywhere. There are, without doubt dazzling places, in abundance, preserved beyond time and space once you get there, but it is the distance and the starting point that are indeed discouraging. Regardless of whether we are in Tamil Nadu in the south, or any state of the North, East or West the problem of getting out there is the same. Roads, access and communications are not usually the most typical of an "emerging" country.

It is true that this also happens in many other places in the world but here, in India, the big challenge for anyone who wants to get around and see these seductive places, is not so much getting there but about how not to become a victim of time and its course. The even bigger challenge is how to stop it! Or better, how to ally with it…go along with the changing rhythms of Time's unstoppable flow! Given the distance from home to work place, circumstances force the common man, to spend half his life going back and forth in trains, buses, metros, rickshaws…or a crazy mix of all of them. One of the security guards at the studio, an elderly man about to retire, who for some reason smiled at me every day, but with whom I could not speak because of the language problem, lived in Mathura, I was told. This pilgrimage city is about 180 kms south of Delhi, in the direction of Agra. The journey was a real nightmare even for those who were accustomed to it. The guard would spend two hours at least to come and as many if not more, to return. Besides which he had to spend a good part of his meagre salary on the travel. But at least the blue uniform gave him a certain status. Difficult as it may be, someone should undertake a study on how to reconcile the places of work and residence and how to humanize that leap.

Yes! This problem, of getting to a place or from it, is tremendous in most cities, but here it acquires distressing proportions. Anyone who has been here, knows that there are incredibly interesting places, from temples, caves, palaces, gardens, jungles, beaches, valleys, and all the etc. that you want, in the four cardinal points of the country. But how do you get to them? How can one say, I am here! It is also true that something is gained in this ultra-congested 21st century, because sometimes one has in certain parts of India the feeling of being really far from everything. And sometimes, just sometimes it offers the soothing sensation of being "lost" and "untraceable."

What makes these places so inaccessible? The first reason that comes to mind, is the lack of directions, of infrastructures, and reliable information. This leads to all kinds of unexpected diversions in the journey, turning any search into an obstacle race. For example, the official *protestodrom* of Jantar Mantar. From the first day I drove to the studio I noticed how crowded it was. And subsequently found that almost every day of the year there was a demonstration there. No dearth of causes or their protagonists! Yes! The analogy that best defines travelling in India is that of a steeplechase! As in these races, competitors must get over the obstacles in the shortest time possible…only here there are no rules. The only one perhaps is to avoid giving a brush, a scrape or a dent, even in the riskiest overtaking maneuvers, much to the horror and surprise of visitors and newcomers to the land.

It is astonishing, for example, how traffic is stopped on any street, at any time, without any forewarning, because a minister or a visiting foreign dignitary is passing through. It makes all of central New Delhi into an impassable chaos. It happens regularly because VIP visits of all kinds are constant. At times, because of the traffic, the city appears to me as a jungle indeed! Sometimes when repeated detours are made, one ends up arriving at the same place! A good driver is therefore essential in the capital and also throughout India! It is not an exaggeration to say that it would take me many days of abstaining from food if that were the only way to employ a driver! To be honest, it can be a risky proposition! The first one I had, Ravindra, was not exactly a Virgil who would drive me through the hells to get out of them. Rather he seemed to want to remain in them. If I have to be accurate in my assessment, he was a true brigand from Bihar. I do not find anything new in this. As is known, quite a few politicians of that State are leaving or entering jail for corruption or other violent acts. And that, when there is prohibition, meaning alcohol is banned, no alcohol is available there! It is one of the several "dry" states where you cannot drink a single drop, even of beer. I"d rather not think what it would be like if there was a bar at every corner!

On several occasions, I have had to give up the idea of attending an event after accepting the invitation, all because of being stuck for more than an hour in a traffic jam. One afternoon during the initial months, I wanted to go to a presentation at the Embassy of Peru. It was to be held in Vasant Vihar, like several other activities of the Latino community that I attended. Despite the fact that I had left the studio with enough time on hand, after almost two hours in traffic I had to give up and turn around practically at the door. It was a difficult and unfortunate decision, like many others, but it made no sense to arrive so late for the event, almost when it was over. Suffering a panic attack, big or small, at not being on time, was a natural consequence.

It is for this reason that many invitations to places like Noida, Saket, or Gurgaon, where some ambassadors' residences, five—star hotels and shopping malls have shifted, meant a displacement of at least two hours from the centre of Delhi. In reality, the capital is nothing but an aggregate of satellite cities, linked by messy, even dangerous half-finished roads and flyovers, with little continuity and fluidity between them. The extreme traffic converts them into watertight compartments and neighbourhoods! The reason for all this is, it can be said, is that after a slow lethargic near vegetal growth over generations, the country has experienced a sudden and rapid spurt since the early 1990s, the consequences of which are not yet very clear or settled, especially with regard to the general good or welfare of the people. It is as if an immense wagon, which always marched at the speed of a bullock cart, suddenly had a turbo engine installed, The axles, the wheels, the entire structure could not withstand it. There are too many internal contradictions! Except the big cities, and some privileged regions such as Punjab and Maharashtra, most of the other parts live and breathe, let's say, in the 19th century, but at the same time they gasp and pant for breath in the 21st century. Or at least they want to desperately, like in a car race, or in a derby, in a staggering technological and cultural leap. Of course they have historical roots to do it, but gaps, brutal mismatches between the majority of the population and the rich minority, is what tears the immense canvas, reduces the large tapestry, to tatters. "Everyone will arrive!"—someone told me once, who of course, had "arrived" at a comfortable life situation. That reminded me of Buddha Maitreya, the "Buddha of the future", and his compassionate willingness to delay enlightenment until the last of the living beings had been released. But now there are very few who would willingly delay their own arrival.

During the long hours spent in the car I had several interesting conversations with Ashwin, my second driver, who recited sacred texts, and according to himself, was a great reader of the palm. I never got him to read mine, but I learned from others, whose palms he had read, of his unique prowess. One such conversation was on what has changed in India in recent times, especially for the generations that grew up after the "reforms" of 1991.

"Without a doubt it has improved the economy and production, but before the fall of the Soviet Bloc (in 1989) we were more 'happy' and respectful of dharma. Now everyone is running only after the money. They do not question what they will do when they have everything and get bored, after having betrayed a thousand times. They do not even think about it!" He continued after my response, "Any madness is allowed to the new rich—they are by definition the first to pass anywhere by force of influence and strength of currency notes, in 'eating up the world', and no one can question it."

What he told me and I saw for myself, it happens, unfortunately, in the Middle East and other places on the planet as well, that if driving a good car, you can afford any barbarity in the street. The subjugators that the new rich are.

Whenever I saw a Porsche, a Lamborghini, or any other Italian "dream" supercar in the Sundar Nagar colony, not very often, no doubt, I wondered which roads they would run on. A deep unseen pothole, an animal or a person crossing unexpectedly, a vehicle stopped in the middle of the road at night, with the lights off. All this, which is more the rule than the exception, would be deadly at a certain speed. I must state that I did not see those cars on any out of the way road, or neighbourhood that was not in this or that privileged colony. Except certain points or very specific enclaves, in few places on Earth can one find the activities of the nouveau riche more out of sync with their environment, with the rest of their fellow citizens. Examples of these brutal contrasts are seen in the flashy commercial malls, such as DLF Emporium in Delhi or The Palladium of Mumbai, next to the shops of Chanel and Armani, so beloved of the new Indian wealthy class located in Vasant Kunj, a few metres from the most abject poverty.

One of the most visible cases of this mismatch, taken to absurd limits, was what I encountered at the airport in Kochi (Cochin) in Kerala, on the return journey to New Delhi. As it often happens on domestic flights with the national carrier, they are inordinately delayed, the delays sometimes becoming interminable. Why does the national airline always suffer from these delays on internal flights, while private airlines tend to be punctual? It's funny, that in a modern and large airport like this one, with many tourists almost all year round, there is no restaurant where you can eat little more than a vegetable sandwich sitting on a fragile plastic chair. However, there is a "jewellery shop" with a wide assortment of costume jewellery, and a large umbrella store, required only in the monsoon season between June and September. And we were in February! Of course, there was no alcohol available, as is common in the vast majority of public places, except for some restaurants in large cities. And the luxury hotels. Perhaps the only exception I can give testimony to is Pune, one of the few airports where there was a totally "western" bar. And yet…surprise! It was not full of drunks! Which is what seems to be the government's fear. Which country which is officially non-Muslim has entire states without a single drop of alcohol available, as in Bihar and Gujarat? How is it possible to prevent anyone from drinking? The dry day, of which the year has many, annoyingly charts the most diverse religious and political festivities, making it difficult for the foreign traveller to endure the hardships of Indian tourism without being able to cheer the food, even with a modest Kingfisher beer.

Like the angry god Saturn of Roman and Greek mythology, who eats his own children, his own works, Time *or Kala,* here is the great devourer who rages. Going back to work places, or going to solve some bureaucratic paperwork, are not purely mechanical chores like in any other part of the globe. It is always going to the unknown, into the jaws of *Kala*, and any unforeseen element can eternalize our exit, however simple it may seem at the start. The only certainty about any formality or procedure is that there will be some problem, with rectifiable ease, such as correcting a name or date. But with less luck, it could involve a long chain of new procedures, signatures, and documents. The whole day is lost in doing two or three simple things that elsewhere would not take more than an hour! However, as time in the West is accelerating with age, here it slows down. It seems that people who manage adulthood, enter into a perpetual state of immanence, of a sustained although precarious eternity. The day, the 24 hours, become in India unfathomable, unpredictable; one can never take anything for granted because at any moment something unexpected can happen, a small or great tragedy that will make us lose the desired pace. Between the obligatory tasks, starting with domestic purchases, made inconvenient by the absence of supermarkets, and the small acts of socializing, add up vertiginously, and time—the hours and the days—runs through our fingers like fine sand.

To compensate for the chaos of traffic and other irritants, one of the greatest pleasures I was able to get in this country, apart from the exquisite curries and visits to some special tourist sites, was the superior pleasure of the most divine Indian music! Evening concerts at various official venues such as the India Habitat Centre, Kamani Auditorium, or the India International Centre, around seven in the evenings, fitted in perfectly with the end of my work day and were the best complement imaginable before retiring to rest. Whether it was Hindustani or the Carnatic, whether it was the qawwali or the ghazal, almost every evening during the week I used to attend recitals of classical Indian music in its most varied genres, both vocal and instrumental. Very soon I was able to distinguish aspects and basic themes of the different genres that were previously totally unknown to me. I was not instructed by anyone in particular to judge and appreciate the styles. It was mostly through some of my own readings, conversations with a few musicians I knew, such as the sitarist Nishat Khan, along with my insatiable desire to hear as many concerts as possible, that helped me to make certain observations and conclusions. My delight was in a sense, directly proportional to the numerous problems I had to deal with at that point.

But when finally installed in a seat, and I could concentrate on the music itself, a goal often difficult to achieve because of the annoying environmental noises and the incessant movement of the audience around the hall or auditorium, the joy was insurmountable.

What happens really is that concerts in India are not just concerts, they have a broad social and ceremonial liturgy that is absent elsewhere in the world, definitely in the West. There the listener usually goes to focus "only" and exclusively on music. The practice in this country, where there are no music academies, is for the apprentice to approach a reputed musician with a school created around him. He will then become a beloved and respected guru for the rest of the life of aspiring musicians, be they singers or instrumentalists. He remains revered even after death. In many cases, the ornately framed photograph of the deceased master presides over the recital, organized in his memory and honour. The consolidated system of musical education has a particular family as its only context. But this is an extended family, not just biological, like the ashram, in what is known as Gharana: Shahjahanpur Gharana, Fatehpur Gharana and others. Endorsed by countless generations, this practice is based on the old *gurukula*, an ingrained learning tradition. If one feels the spiritual and emotional call to a particular teacher, he leaves his natural family, to live with co-disciples in a place that could be far away from his hometown and stays there for as long as it takes to acquire mastery over a particular vocal or instrumental art. And eventually he himself will become a master of his specialty, a virtuoso who would extend all through India and the world, the good name of his gharana, his instructor, and his own.

Coming from this indisputable atmosphere of devotion, the student/artiste of the evening, before embarking on his performance offers the greatest consideration of his respect to his teacher, with the obligatory words of greeting and introduction, and touching the teacher's feet in a symbolic act of veneration if the teacher is present in the room. Everything happens after the prescriptive lighting of the wicks in the oil lamp of either brass or bronze. Then on many occasions a gift of flowers and/or shawls are presented to the artiste before he/she settles down on the wooden stage to play or sing or dance. While I was quick to notice the veneration and the high degree of mastery of the musicians over their instruments, my initial observation was that in the concerts many people did not actually hear what was going on on the stage in front of them. Of course there are some who are connoisseurs, but they are a minority. Part of the audience is relatives, children, nephews, parents, cousins…some perhaps coming from afar, and are only concerned with clicking photos, arranging for drinking water, and taking care of thousand other contingencies such as the sound and microphone arrangement.

My surprise was abundant in the first recitals that I went to, because suffering but unshaken, the musicians continued with their labour of love, undoubtedly already accustomed to finding themselves in an intermediary trance between their necessary concentration and the frantic auditorium where movement wouldn't stop. Despite the constant getting up and sitting down of the audience, the coming and going, especially in the front rows, the clicks of the cameras, and the loud comments which should have ruined the concert for a Western "barbarian" like me, it didn't bother anyone else! These are European niceties, Western niceties, they must have thought, when sometimes I made my displeasure obvious, particularly drawing the attention of the most bored to maintain silence. I almost stopped doing that when I realized that the movement and the noises were a widespread habit. Silence! Concentration! Self restraint! That was what I tried to ask of them. It's funny! I was asking them for just what a Westerner thinks is genuinely Indian! Fortunately, it wasn't often that mothers and other members of the audience who are there to pass time, leave the kids to run down the aisles, or on to the stage, practicing all kinds of screaming and gurgling that hardly rhymes with the elevated music.

In spite of all these irritants I was attending, faithfully, concerts almost every evening! And I did it always armed with a jacket in my hand. The reason is clear! Even in winter, air conditioning is usually at full blast, hence the constant coughs that are heard from the four corners of the auditorium. At times the stream of cold air forced me to change seats, and I would look for another place where the cold did not freeze my neck and head. How can one move from the 40 degrees of the street at times, to less than 20, by crossing only one door? It is not just the low temperature setting of the air conditioning, it is also the fan that is kept at full blast, whether it is in an elevator, the ceiling of a shop or in an office! This unquestioned habit of the accelerated fan blades give rise to more than one comic situation! I once witnessed the blast of wind from the heights lift the cap off a tabla player's head, in the middle of a concert, forcing him to run after it.

This is not a joke, neither the air at full blast, nor the lack of attention or focus one breathes everywhere: people looking at their phones, some twisting their heads in all directions, either looking for someone or to see who all are present, and of course, couples talking uninhibitedly, as if the concert was not going well with them, as if it were by accident that they had entered there, for many of these concerts are entirely gratis. Often I too looked, one by one, at the audience. Few were really attentive to the music! How was it that hardly anyone in the room was concentrating on the sounds that they had supposedly come to hear? Do they not care at all about the content? Was it always like this? Or perhaps something more recent?

I was struck by the continuous "click" of the cameras, not just professional photographers hired by the media but spontaneous amateurs. I wondered where the obsession came from, because in any case thousands of images of any event are always available. Would they ever look at these photographs again another day? I can understand this obsession about dance, where each instant changes the gestures of the performers, the expressions of body, the colours, the perspective of the costumes swirling to the movement, the lights. But can someone explain to me what sense it makes to take hundreds of pictures throughout the concert, of three or four people sitting statically, focused on their instruments? No doubt this accelerated world of mobile phones and computers has decentered and maddened all—not just here, in all parts of the world. Nothing is any longer as it was until a few years ago, when life moved in a modest scale, at a slow, even pace, here in India.

I did not give up though. I sought these concerts out, and tried to get some relaxation from them confronting the noise, and at times the bothersome attitude of the viewers, with patience and tolerance. I reminded myself many times that it was here that Yoga was born! It is here that concentration has naturally emerged in the most subtle physical processes of the body during meditation, as well as the most refined distinctions in the deep recesses of the mind. And these have led to the thousand and one Sanskrit terms for the fleeting nuances of the observing consciousness. But these reflections, and others, in which I got lost, were of little worth there, sitting as a striving spectator, who sometimes achieved the impossible feat of snatching a few seconds or even minutes of silence!

Despite all these drawbacks, most of the time I would leave the hall almost floating, beyond myself, transcended! That meant that I had felt something in there, not only special, but really unique. I had absorbed with my whole body and mind a privileged point of fusion with a multitude of elements, something that rarely happens. The result was a sense of detachment from my body even as I sat there, the world in an enigmatic equilibrium, allowing for a sort of vertical flight, and a horizontal spread at the same time, perhaps of the soul. Transcendence and immanence experienced in an eternal now! One doesn't know a priori, if this unique perception will happen on a particular day. No doubt the name and reputation of a musician assures a good performance, but it's not always like that! The interpretation may be correct but cold, well planned but not quite uplifting. Whereas a young unknown artiste coming from some far off place plays, or sometimes sings, with such spirit that he reaches levels that even he is not aware of. In its invisibility and its profound effects, this poetic immensity of sound we call music is the most immaterial of the arts, the most intangible. And that is why it is linked profoundly to the spiritual evolution of the one practicing it.

All through the four long years I ended up living in New Delhi, those concerts were the one thing I would not deny myself. In them, my mood and well-being ascended limitlessly, reaching at times a great mental and spiritual euphoria. It was like I was deprived of water, or air to breathe, if four or five days passed without my being able to attend a recital, be it vocal, sarod, sitar, bansuri or sarangi… it didn't matter! It was always a mystery whether that miraculous communication would happen or not, and indeed, it does not always happen, yet more often than not, it does. The musician starts playing slowly, always gradually tuning his voice where appropriate, and with every note imperceptibly raising the pace and intensity, until reaching a series of flashpoints, repeated into climax, concluded by a final one, which sometimes seems never to come… With hardly an interruption, other than to occasionally tune the instrument, or to make a brief comment, the exploration of a raga extends for an hour or more. In this way, the singer or instrumentalist gets to make himself a channel of transmission from a faraway place, wherefrom comes the root of the sounds. What begins as a personal affair, pertaining to a single name, or a particular school, ends up becoming a lifetime legacy for all those who listen with care. The objective achieved, the concert concludes as a burst of pure energy which seems to breathe deeply into the four walls that embrace it, as if they were a large lung.

Music is the true, authentic spiritual path. It arises from the primordial vibration AUM, and goes back to it, obtaining in this transit a great detachment and peace of mind. When we let ourselves go in it, that trance, puts us in parallel with the cosmic waves that unite heaven and earth. Every note and every silence is a step towards liberation, moksha. Therefore, for many Indian philosophers this sound represents the divinity itself—*nada-brahma*.

In this way liberation becomes the overcoming of matter and energy, represented by the instruments and voice. Despite their solidity, the instrument or the voice achieves something entirely immaterial, beyond the samsara of existence, whose identity is coded in everyday wear and tear, in suffering and decay. When music reaches levels of excellence in voice or in the hands of someone privileged, it is able to penetrate like a perforator, into the ultimate limits of our divine nature. Therefore, it is yoga, which genuinely means "union" that goes beyond physical or mental positions. It also goes beyond those who listen to such music, forming in the act, a single and indivisible body through one of our senses: hearing, and through it fusing us with the ultimate source of fulfilment and happiness.

The first music of this subcontinent starts from the wet mist of the forests, and later from the porticoes of the temples. It then acquires its first formalization in the days of *Sama* and *Yajur* Vedas. Such were the texts that between 1500 and 500 years before Christ, they sought to regulate the hymns and mantras concerning rituals and prayers of Indo-European solar religion coming from the West. The same one, that evolving with local elements and a thousand different tendencies, from the ultra-theistic to atheistic, centuries later we now know as Hinduism. In the time of the Guptas (3rd century BC), and with the passing of generations, a certain type or canon of classical music would be formed, which, patronized by the courts and powers that be, would not, any more, be purely religious or folk. The road was paved for the formation of Hindustani music, born with Iranian contributions in Mughal durbars or courts. At least in the north, it is this music that is today mostly heard in the "cultured" evenings, a music that achieved an intimate and dazzling mix of foreign and indigenous Indian elements. Amir Khusrau is undoubtedly the ultimate example of a spiritual poet, who was at the same time a courtier too, an extremely cultured poet, who drank from Indian and Persian sources, and was the creator of the style *Khayal*, with its immense dreaminess and emotionality.

As the first and most important genre, the raga stands out, and its pillars are melody and rhythm. The whole universe of Indian music is constructed on the basis of the scale or *sargama*, which has a range of seven notes (abbreviated as sa, re, ga, ma, pa, dha, and ni). This much is as with Western music. However unlike it, which reaches till the semitone, Indian music has quarter tones, and therefore one could say twice the precision. With an array of variations, based on three main speeds, this music harbours a variety of rhythms. If the rhythmic cycles or tala constitute the skeleton of the ragas, the melodic scales make up the body. What is truly peculiar to this musical tradition, which so filled up my life in those years in New Delhi, lies mainly in the use of intervals and scales unusual in other types of music. Conceived by leading instrumentalists to gradually raise mental states linked to a particular time of day, or time of year, the ragas were composed in the past as backbones of all Indian music. From the Sanskrit *ranj*, "colour", its meaning points to something tinged with a certain emotion, by a definite feeling—nostalgia, passion, loss, awakening, hope… Hence its sensitive range, its "colour" like an ink discharged on water, impacting the listener like a spiritual and emotional dye.

From the mists of the past shines the famous and enigmatic Tansen, a musician from Central India who apparently lived during almost the entire 16th century including the prodigious reign of Emperor Akbar, whose favourite singer he was, and was named one of the nine Navaratnas, or "jewels" of the Mughal empire. He shared the time of the legendary poet and philosopher Tulsidas, and of Meerabai, the mystic devotee of Krishna. In the manner of an Indian Orpheus (of Greek mythology), marvels are attributed to him, like he knew how to transmit a special peace to beings, working wonders in them, as well as in animals and the elements too. Like Akbar or his ill-fated grandson, Dara Shikoh, Tansen symbolizes a rich syncretic culture that emerged as a rare plant, as beautiful as fragile, between worlds as diverse as Hindu and Islamic. While, except in certain minds and hearts, it did not come to see the light of day in the form of a religion, it did signify a lofty merger with the best of the "two oceans", which, for example, fructified in the architecture of the great Mughal buildings. It was Aurangzeb who banned any form of music and dance in the court. In addition, he indulged in other acts of extremism, like murdering his own brother to seize power. Thereafter, Hindustani classical music fell into a brutal decay, experiencing a rebirth only in the late 19th century, and in the 20th century spreading around the world, with musicians like Ravi Shankar or Ustad Bismillah Khan, and later, Lakshminarayan Subramaniam, receiving admiration. Yes! Any consideration of India and its culture passes first through its music! It is a true reflection of most intense spirituality, deposited layer after layer on ragas, over the centuries. And perhaps nowhere else on Earth have so many myths, philosophies, and religions developed that have sound, vibration, the beyond and the here of words as origin and manifestation of all that exists. Everything here is music! Everything starts and ends with it! It is far more complex than we in the West understand it. *Sangita,* a notion that is untranslatable and identifies with an array of vocal and instrumental music, and dance.

The king instrument of Indian music is definitely the sitar! According to legend, the great poet Amir Khusrau was the one who created it to the delight of posterity, in the 13th century. In fact, it is a long-mast lute, with a strong metallic sound, which both in appearance and sound is halfway between the Indian veena, and the Persian tambura, although reinvented now into a purely Indian instrument! This great instrument has a total of 26 steel strings, which are pulsed by a *mizrab* spike. Four of them serve the melody, and three to the harmonic and rhythmic accompaniment, vibrating the other 19 by sympathy, with a great resonance and solidity of sound.

The glissando are one of the most typical and attractive movements of the sitar, in which the musician slides his left hand through the mast, passing quickly from one tone to another more serious, or more acute. And in that transit between them you can hear the whole range of their intermediate sounds.

The veena, associated with Saraswati, the goddess of music and learning, is perhaps the most purely Indian instrument. That is why the most popular form of the instrument is known as Saraswati veena. The four main strings, which run through the 24 frets, are played with the fingertips. To them are added three auxiliary strings, offering the rhythmic accompaniment.

The sarangi, known as the violin of India, has, in addition to the four strings of wire that are played, another twenty, which vibrate by sympathy, with a sound very rich in harmonics. That's what gives it its name—*sa-rang*, with colour.

In contrast to the sharp, but sweet and relaxing sound plot of the sitar, the sarod has a deep and internalized register. It is also a stringed instrument, with a sound as strange as it is attractive, and is the product of several previous ones, such as the Persian *rabab*. Although it did not exist in ancient India, today it is well known and established. With a fretless metal mast, the sarod has between 20 and 25 strings, five of them for the melody, ten sympathetic and others for resonance.

The tambura or tanpura, is an instrument similar in form to the sitar, in charge of keeping constant the basic tone *sa*, to show the ground on which the singer and the instrumentalists have to walk along their flight, always with the feet on earth.

The tabla, the great Indian paired drum/double drum, is not only used as a rhythmic accompaniment for other instruments, or vocalists it works also as a solo instrument. The sounds of the tabla, as nuanced as they are forceful, as metallic as they are deep, come from two drums. The small one, or *dagga*, that is struck with the fingers, the palm and wrist of the left hand, and the thick one, or *siddha*, that is caressed with the fingers and the palm of the right.

The bansuri, the flute made of bamboo, light and without knots, with six or seven holes, is associated with the landscape and the life of the farmers, as well as with the loves of Krishna and Radha.

Although the violin is not a traditional Indian instrument, introduced as it was in the 19th century from Europe, today it is part of many recitals, both as accompaniment, and as a solo instrument. After starting as a secondary instrument, dialoguing with a main musician, it arrived at the place where it currently is, with dazzling scales and arpeggios, thanks in large part to L.V. Subramaniam.

But to come back to the city which was my home now, a brief history of New Delhi, its planning and its construction will be in order. It has been only ninety years since New Delhi was inaugurated. As is known to those who are interested in history and are aware of its course changes, the original plan was that New Delhi, this compound name that is well-known and evident, would lie to the north of the old capital, Shahjahanabad. In fact, the British cantonment with all its institutions, military and political, from the Supreme Court to the cemetery, was in the area then, now known as Civil Lines. It was there that King George V laid the foundation stone of the city, in the Durbar celebrated with great pomp at the end of 1911. At that time the king officially announced what was already known for some time, that the British imperial headquarters in India would be transferred from Calcutta to this precise location, which, from the mythical Indraprashtha, had often been an important capital of sultanates, kingdoms and empires over the centuries. The reason for the relocation was clear. From the late 18th century, the British had spread over much of what is now India, militarily taking over what until then had been only a commercial consortium—the British East India Company. When they came to Delhi in the early 19th century, and placed the Mughal emperor under their power, after the revolt of 1857, and forced him into exile in Burma, they needed a new capital city. Delhi was more centrally located, in the north of India, whereas Calcutta was on the eastern coast, too far for ships coming in from London. Mumbai port was closer to Delhi as well.

The idea of locating the new city in the north, however, took an unexpected course when the chief architect of the project, the already famous Edwin Lutyens (1869–1944), arrived. The proximity of the river Yamuna, with the infinite swarms of mosquitoes its stagnant backwaters could produce, and the possible diseases that they could undoubtedly give rise to, deterred Lutyens from the very first moment. He did not take the presupposed plans as immovable, even though the monarch himself had placed the first stone with great pomp and ceremony. For several days he devoted himself to riding on elephant back, through the possible enclaves in search of the site for the future capital of the British Empire of India. He was accompanied by the second architect appointed to the project, Herbert Baker (1862–1946). In Sir Lutyens" mind the new capital had to be spread over an immense and privileged space. The result of that search, though difficult, was encouraging. He found an area further to the south, near the village of Malcha, in the present area of Chanakyapuri, which seemed much more convenient. Without wasting any time, he wrote a report for London that was well documented and extensive.

In that, he suggested that the city, which he was already visualizing, would stretch from this village to the Old Fort (Purana Qila), on the east-west axis, and from the current Golf Links to what later would be the radial centre of Connaught Place, on the north-south axis. He clearly saw that the Raisina hill, wihch overlooked the entire designated area, would be the place to house the viceroy "s palace, which is now Rashtrapati Bhavan, the headquarters of the President of India.

The new plans sent by the great architect possessed not only a justified but an overwhelming logic. Considering that this was a meridian change of location, approval for it came relatively quickly for those times. The Durbar had taken place on 12 December 1911, and by early 1913, the ad hoc committee (Town Planning Commission) that was created, had already decided that the capital should be located not north but south of Shahjahanabad, as the capital of the great Mughal Shah Jahan (Emperor Akbar's grandson), was then called. This carried advantages in every way over the first location, starting with the fact that it would offer an image of novelty for the projected British imperial seat, with hardly any vestiges of the past in that area, no reminders of other rulers, except for the Lodi tombs. Also the land there was not only more suitable than in the north, but also more even and cheaper when adding up the expropriations. These were not many, for sure, since the one who offered most of this land was the Maharaja of Jaipur, whose ancestor had received the lands from the Mughal emperor in a marriage. The current Maharaja gave them graciously to the British as a mark of his respect. The most curious episode from this unexpected change of location, is about how, in the middle of a night in 1913, a cart carried the foundation stone from the Coronation Park where it had been placed by King George V, all the way up to the Raisina Hill. At this spot construction work would soon begin.

With the obelisk that recalls this fact, covered in weeds, Coronation Park to the north of Delhi still exists, with an obelisk that commemorates the 1911 Durbar. Prior to this, the grand assembly, or Imperial Durbar had been convened, on two previous occasions, in 1877 and 1903. The first happened as a consequence of the fact that the previous year, in 1876, the British Parliament, on Disraeli's proposal, had named Queen Victoria Empress of India. Thus, after the bloody catharsis that the revolt of 1857 meant for both communities, the British Crown was made heir to the already diminished Mughal Imperial House. In the manner of the Mughal Durbar, Indian princes were made direct subjects of Victoria, then Queen, and now Empress. The British government acted de facto as an "expanded" East Indian Company. Viceroy Lytton was the highest representative at the ceremony, which attempted to combine the two paraphernalia—the Indian and the British. In the following event, in 1903, on the occasion of the accession of Edward VII, Lord Lytton's successor, Lord Curzon, had the decency to sit with the Maharajas in the amphitheater. For this ceremony, there did arrive a representative from London, the Duke of Connaught, Victoria's youngest son, who years later would give his name to the capital's "down town" area.

None of these previous Durbars was attended by King George V, the only British emperor, who with his wife and consort Mary, came to visit a fraction of his vast eastern realms. The king said in his speech that the city, as well as public buildings, would be built "with the greatest care and know-how". It would be, he assured, an "Anglo-Indian Rome," which would accommodate about 65,000 people. Following the planning of the great capitals erected between the end of the 19th and early 20th centuries, such as Paris, Washington or Pretoria, it would be built for eternity, with one of the most amazing residences—that of the Viceroy.

The great meeting was held in the grand Mughal tradition, under a golden dome and a long roof that brought together the thousand chosen ones, many of them senior British officials, along with representatives of many royal houses of India such as Jaipur, Orissa, Hyderabad, Bengal, Bihar, Baroda, Patiala and more. Outside, under the open sky, ten lakh Indians flocked to the ceremony, in an immense prepared space where numerous events had been scheduled. In the past, these ceremonial meetings were based on an exchange of gifts, such as jewellery, exotic animals, or exquisite weapons, through which the sovereignty of the emperor was accepted, and the authority of the local rulers sanctioned. For this occasion, some thirty thousand commemorative silver medals were minted, mostly for the incumbents of British regiments, as well as some in gold for the maharajas and officers of higher rank.

The new capital of the Raj boasted of being one of the oldest cities in the world, from Indraprashtha, founded, as per the Mahabharata, by the Pandavas, to the Mughal Shahjahanabad, through the Sultanate of Delhi, and Lalkot, Siri, Tughlakabad, and Ferozabad, which were Muslim. All of them, according to recounts, add up to a total of 7, 12 or 21 cities. It wasn't, therefore, a new capital at all, although the open place where it would finally be located would be a new city with wide green avenues, and an impressive space between the India Gate and the Palace of the Viceroy. The two huge Secretariats on either side, which housed the headquarters of the British Empire, were built by Baker, chosen by Lutyens for his wide experience in South Africa. They had certain Indian elements, such as elevations on plinths, and *chattris* or domed pavilions. These two buildings, advanced about a hundred metres from the main building, and dominated the entire landscape on Raisina Hill. It was Baker who also built the Parliament, with its two halls, the Lok Sabha (Council of the People), and the Rajya Sabha (Council of the States).

On his part, Lutyens, who had extensive experience particularly in English country estates, did not show any marked influence of Indian architecture, except vaguely, in the materials—red Rajasthan limestone used as signature in Mughal constructions. The unique architectural concessions were the *chattris* in certain corners of the complex, and the central dome, which seems to reproduce the great Buddhist stupa at Sanchi. Besides the main building of the viceroy's residence, Lutyens would undertake the development of New Delhi, and India Gate. Around this vast space, he built the palaces of some of the most famous maharajas, of Baroda and of Hyderabad, in addition to the National Archives building, then called Imperial Records Department.

Thus the two main axes were as follows—the perpendicular avenue, Janpath, between Connaught Circus and Safdarjung's Tomb and on the other side, Rajpath, between the great palace, crowning the mound, and India Gate, which represented a symbolic entrance to the entire Palace of the Viceroy from the river.

All this, of course, did not come up overnight, although it was relatively fast for the colossal and extensive volume of work, similar to what would be undertaken some decades later, for example, in Brasilia. The difference is that the structures and materials chosen for the Indian project was conceived as "for eternity". Once the decision on the exact location was made almost everything was undertaken between 1913 and 1931, when finally, New Delhi was inaugurated, although without a royal presence. It was a garden city, built on the basis of hexagons, and especially triangles in its design, figures that had already played an important role in Mughal architecture. It is incredible that such an achievement, that great Anglo-Indian Rome, the most impressive Asian city to be built in many generations, lasted the British only 16 years, from 1931 to 1947, losing her to Independence. New Delhi was planned to last for centuries! And they barely enjoyed her for those short years. That's right, there it remained for future generations of Indians to enjoy!

Located between Old and New Delhi, Connaught Circus is about three kilometres away from the main axis of the city, equidistant from India Gate and the Palace. The venue for this important commercial and social area had originally been a small forest of Cassia (*kikar)* trees, and was projected at the beginning to be composed of six blocks, with 585 pillars in the inner circle, and 1021 double pillars in the outer one. It was the Duke of Connaught who in his second stay laid the foundation stone of this complex, as also of Parliament, giving his name in 1921 to this shopping complex designed in concentric circles, and built by R.T. Russell (1888–1972). Its most characteristic features are the Palladian arches and thick white columns. This renowned architect also made the main Eastern and Western Courts on both sides of Queensway, the principal street radiating from the Circus, now known as Janpath. Russell, who had worked for the British service in Mesopotamia and elsewhere, was active in New Delhi until 1933. In addition to this hub of incessant activity, currently the true city centre, Russell conceived the large bungalow, Teen Murti Bhavan (Flagstaff House), for the Commander-in-Chief of the British Army in India, which after independence was occupied by the then Prime Minister Jawaharlal Nehru (1888–1972). Many other buildings, offices and colonial mansions extend the list of his works, including Safdarjung airport the first civilian airport, and the predecessor of the current Indira Gandhi International Airport.

Connaught Place in New Delhi represents the only big centralized and identifiable "down town". But gradually, it ceased to be the elegant centre of the capital, with the best tailors and shirt makers, as other scattered commercial venues like Khan Market, INA, Hauz Khas, etc. grew. However a dense core is getting formed there, of restaurants, fast food joints, clothing establishments, and electronic goods shops, and it does not stop growing.

It is surprising how this place is seeing a resurgence thanks to the metro and numerous means of communication that connect it to other ends of the city, and trying, once again to assert itself as the radial center of that dreamed "Rome of the 20th century".

Maybe it does not surprise those who live in this city, already accustomed to this curious and ubiquitous presence of dogs. But for anyone who happens to come to New Delhi the large number of stray dogs that roam everywhere is undoubtedly striking. It is surprising how they behave—they are seen in the parks, lounging on the benches, at the doors of the houses that are not theirs, like passers-by, on all the roads of the city, wide and narrow. Few places in the world I think are there so many dogs per square metre! It does not happen with cows, who also indolently roam around without disturbing or interfering with anyone, living in a kind of parallel reality of another timeless time. But drifting dogs, with sad and pensive looks, wander through the streets, their eyes reflecting a deep existential anguish. Beyond their dirty and miserable appearance it is as if they were aware of dragging a negative karma, as if they knew that they have to wait a long time until their next reincarnation. Yes, it is as if in some way they are aware of paying a high price for a past life that necessarily must have been very bad. They seem to know for sure that they have ahead of them many existences on this earth still, seeing themselves sacrificed, with a suffering forced unto them by virtue of their destiny.

Basking in the sun in winters, they sleep and yawn all day, and do the same the rest of the year, but in the shade. In the night's cool, however, they become energized, barking and bothering anyone who passes by. Many people are accustomed to this and are not unduly perturbed by it. It wouldn't matter if they did not attack and bite pedestrians, who must immediately be administered the rabies vaccine. But then, surprised by their aggressiveness, and by the risk that many of them pose given their pathetic condition, I asked the head of the Residents' Association of Sundar Nagar, my neighbourhood, in writing, if there existed, as in Europe something like kennels. Days later, the predictable answer was that they do not exist, even though the number and menace of stray dogs continues to grow relentlessly. Something that also drew my particular attention in this respect, was the fact that there were hardly any bitches… Or at least they were not visible. I was intrigued by this and thought, they must be somewhere, in hiding or hidden! For, after all, if there were no females, there would be no dogs! Such an obvious and reassuring conclusion!

Anyone who is new to this country, is likely to be intrigued by the feudal post-capitalism one witnesses here in India. What does one call it? Plutocracy? Clientelist capitalism? It is a rather peculiar economic structure of society. The management framework of companies, banks, industries, and large corporations has not been fully opened up organically to the society.

Many of the financial and commercial enterprises that are successful are often in family hands. Unlike the other parts of the world, large companies are run and controlled by well identified names of family members or founders. There are few shareholders from among the public or partners in these enterprises. While the family is the nucleus of the Indian economic fabric, and could be a solid pillar of security and stability, it presents an evident problem of opacity, of secrecy, along with almost zero participation of its employees in the decisions and benefits. What dominates is crony capitalism, one in which the businesses run on hidden paths, different from those of the ordinary market, which happens on the street and in stores. These parallel businesses thrive thanks to the connections with certain officials or politicians, all of whom, for example, can obtain or facilitate entry permits to the country, and subsequent distribution of the goods

As in the time of the gold rush in North America, millionaires and billionaires are proliferating in an accelerated manner, but this does not generate the requisites for an advanced civil society. A large collective that is mostly poor, is unfair, unjust! But it is also inefficient. There is hardly any production or consumption, so there are no advances in the quality of life. And in such circumstances there is hardly any synergy among the various sectors of the economy, which is largely a subsistence economy. Every rich "entrepreneur" does not generate in his direct and indirect employees, concentric circles of wealth; it rather stays strictly in the family! Thus, on the surface of these still waters, where turbulences seldom happen, a kind of economic malaria is generated, typical of the swamps. Retaining virtually all profits in very few hands creates an economy that works like a medieval village, only multiplied a thousand, even a million times. Like a fractal! A village multiplied to infinity! This is something that can be extended to the infrastructures, to the scarce and stagnant services, to the means of communication—the streets, the roads. All of them are obsolete in India, flagrantly insufficient for the number of inhabitants and their needs.

India! This great tide of contrasts between excess and lack, of successive counterpoints without frontiers, which never reconcile! Stretched to its two social extremes, India lives its day to day like two completely different countries. One is that of the big global figures, that of the billionaires connected in their businesses with the most distant places, and the other, the country with one of the lowest per capita incomes on the planet.

While in the scientific field, and in space missions, Indian projects advance at a level close to the developed nations, and in parallel, the economic alliances and the geostrategic games are those of a medium power.

In a list that in recent decades has been growing like a wildfire, there are about 80 billionaires in India. People who have at least a billion dollars! At the end of the last millennium, they captured less than 1 per cent of GDP, and in just a decade they have reached 30 per cent… One hundred persons have more accumulated wealth than 400 million people! Although they certainly have strong pharmaceutical, metallurgical, mining, construction, and telecommunications industries, property, real estate, is by far the greatest wealth. The first of the wealthiest families is perhaps that of Mukesh Ambani (Reliance Industries Ltd), followed, among others, by Sunil Mittal (Bharti Airtel), Keshub Mahindra (Mahindra & Mahindra), Sajjan Jindal (JSW Steel), or Kumar Birla (Grasim). Some occupy bright marble offices with designer Italian furniture; others are in shabby buildings that touch the sordid. This, though, is not indicative of the bulk of the business! They are like new maharajas; They all have great personal talent, but usually they have had a mentor, often their own father, who has helped them to get where they are. Some like Ratan Tata, Aditya Birla or Rahul Bajaj, were among the first wealthy ones. Fortune already came to them from their families, from before Independence. Others, however, came from humble positions, such as Dhirubhai Ambani, the father of this famous family saga, who started as an employee at a gas station.

The gods most adored at the time of undertaking business, to wish that these be auspicious and add wealth to their promoters, are

Ganesha, with the head of an elephant, and Lakshmi. It is specially the latter, with her omnipresent image in small or large temples, where she is daily invoked to manifest herself in all her splendour, thus maintaining a privileged status for herself. Like the Greek Venus, but demure in this case, removed from voluptuousness, Lakshmi always appears serene and erect, as though newly emerged from the waters. Standing on a pink lotus! Surrounded by innumerable precious stones! These were thrown in profusion by the gods and some humans, who wanted her to visit their houses, since wherever Lakshmi passes wealth will also be found. During the autumn festival of lights (Diwali), Indians celebrate this beloved goddess through numerous rituals with candles and lamps of all kinds, as they believe that on that night, between October and November, she will descend from her abode in heaven to bless the most illuminated of the houses.

On the other hand, Vishnu, her divine husband in Hindu mythology, confers on his consort the attributes of continuity, maintenance, and preservation of the order established in the universe. She is the firm incarnation of beauty, charm, and grace. Both in the plane of everyday visible matter, as in the spiritual, she is the goddess of abundance, and prosperity. Altars dedicated to Lakshmi are always loaded with oil, milk, and flowers. But it seems to indicate that the ultimate goal of life is beyond wealth or poverty. It represents, in both cases, achieving the proposed objective. Not in vain, the origin of her Sanskrit name means "goal", "arrival", that is, the outcrop of many elements put into play as life advances. She is not in the beginnings, in the starting points, but in the arrival. Lakshmi. The embodiment of the ultimate goal of existence, which includes material and spiritual prosperity. She possesses four arms and four hands, in which she carries an endless shower of gold and flowers. While the front hands suggest the physical activity of the physical world, the posterior ones symbolize the hidden abilities that lead to the transcendental plane. In all her representations, she is the very image of harmony in life, of the ultimate balance between the tensions of samsara, remaining graceful on her privileged floral float. Donned in red and gold colours, symbols of vitality and prosperity, she appears, always, standing on a pink lotus. Lakshmi thus warns that although the riches of the world are desirable for well-being, these should be enjoyed with a certain detachment, without excess and without obsession. Not in vain, the lotus is a flower of rich symbolism, that grows, that shows up on the surface of the water. And it stays there, floating immaculate before the sight, no matter how much its roots come from the mud and actually feed on the rot…a transfigured rot.

A big open secret in India is that only the private sector works, moved by one or many players without official bureaucratic ties. There alone one can find some efficiency and accountability, as against the public sector, each day more archaic, and more obsolete, like a great plaster skeleton, full of dust. Not even in the medium term, can one foresee a future, with an agile administration that would resolve some things for the most disadvantaged citizens. In the public sphere, only the political part, the very high officials, are well informed and operational. What is the possible way out of this impasse that seems eternalized? The only big and distant hope lies in the fact that leaders, young highly educated innovators, even from the private sector, start engaging in the near future, with a more established stage of growth, not only of their own more immediate individual interests, but of their country! But for this, they must receive salaries which are not so miserable! With the exception of the world of culture, which until now has had a discreet, although continued official support, it seems that all areas are crying out for everything to be privatized. I reiterate that this country manifests the great inoperability, and confers a discontinuity that is ubiquitous throughout. A country that works with two speeds! Like a car that can only march slowly, at the pace of the pedestrian, or runaway, like a racing car…With nothing, no chance of anything in between!

Napoleon, imitated much later by Churchill, said admiringly of China that it was a sleeping giant, but that when it would wake up, it would shake the world. This is already happening! The tremor was not fortunately caused by wars, but by the economy, which today seems to dominate everything without exception. It happened over the last few decades, propitiated by selfless work not bound by schedules, on the part of its citizens, together with the total absence of labour and political rights. So the Chinese are already present as a "Giant awake" in a good part of the planet, in the capitals, the provinces, and the most remote areas in search of resources and fuels: Africa, Latin America, and the Pacific. The others to awaken in this geographical area were Japan and the Southeast Asian Tigers (South Korea, Taiwan, Singapore, Indonesia). Now maybe it's the turn of others more to the West! Is the Indian alarm clock ringing? Its GDP is already in the top five, but the per capita income is still plunged in a bottomless pit—in the 143rd place, a little ahead of Pakistan, which is at 145. India's eventual incorporation into the "emerged" countries that have made the future their own, will not make the world tremble in the same way as is happening with the Chinese. It will undoubtedly be at a slower pace, and for the moment at least, it will incorporate only certain layers of the population. First the rich, and then that elusive "middle class" that is talked about so much, but except in the big cities, is seen so little, and in any case, hasn't really consolidated. What is the barometer to know how many have already ascended to this status of the doubtful middle class? Of course it is not about earning a few dollars a day, and having a motorcycle. The constant contradictions between extreme opulence and misery, between ultra-traditional social habits, and a representative democracy for 1,300 million people, are not resolved. The most privileged areas are in the West, in states such as Punjab or Maharashtra, and the ones that suffer the highest rates of poverty and low growth, are in the East, with Bihar at the top. The Indian case is also, in fact, that of a huge giant asleep for a long time, at least in the international scene as much as in the internal social scene, which thanks to a liberalized economy, is finally waking up. A part of it has actually awakened! Like the hovering image of the floating iceberg, out of it comes a tiny sunny rock, under which lies a great mass of ice, sunk in the dark and cold waters. How many times bigger than the part that has emerged?

For the moment, all the signs of growth and improvement are enormously paradoxical, and ambiguous. If until just twenty years ago India was considered one of the poorest nations on the planet, with famines and natural disasters, in a few decades it has acquired the label of "emergent", thus jumping from the total absence to a certain international visibility, which is not only that of Bollywood. The strong change of rudder, like the turn of a ship of many degrees in full navigation, was given in 1991 by the then Minister of Finance, Manmohan Singh, who would later become Prime Minister. In a declaration of principles, he once said, "The world must understand that India has changed." Gone was the socialism adopted in the fifties and sixties by Nehru, and the state of emergency of Indira Gandhi in the seventies until the drama of her murder in 1984. Spurred by the then recent assassination of Rajiv Gandhi in 1991, Singh took advantage of a deep crisis in India to carry out various structural changes that liberalized the economy of his country.

Singh's determination would be compensated by a nation awaiting measures to be taken in tune with the times, and he would be elected years later, in 2004, as the 14th Prime Minister of India, and then re-elected until 2014. This made him not only the first Sikh who came to that position, but also the only politician after Jawaharlal Nehru who got re-elected.

In spite of all this, of that opening up, and of having reached a mixed economy, with a growing private industry, the radical omnipresence of the State dominating the day to day life of the people still continues. And it is not so much in the rights, but in the duties, in a method still in force since the semi-socialist and ultra-protector Nehru era. Inertia is brutal! As much as we speak of a country that grows at 6 per cent or 7 per cent in a sustained manner, the levels of illiteracy and schooling are extremely high and very low, respectively, in addition to half of its inhabitants subsisting with barely two euros a day. In fact, India is therefore many Indias. It is something like a solar system with many planets, in which some of them are very close to the sun, burning in seas of liquid gold, while others are far away in the outer orbits, such as Saturn or Pluto, and there the light of the central star hardly ever reaches. It is overwhelming that agriculture grew only 2 per cent on average throughout the country in recent years, in contrast to industry and services, which grew by almost 10 per cent. Agriculture, no doubt, is the poor sister of Indian development. For not being able to pay interest on their loans, 200,000 peasants committed suicide in little more than ten years, between 1997 and 2008.

No one doubts that India is a country of exceptions, enriched by innumerable umbilical cords that bind it as much to a timeless past, as to a future that may be fascinating, although beyond common aspirations. For now, only a limited industry in proportion to the volume of its inhabitants, has "emerged". These are to some extent privileged islands, which are found remote from each other, lost in a great archipelago of poverty and underdevelopment. Yes, India is really many Indias! It is perceived as a sea of soap bubbles that float like separate realities, some briskly, and ascending, with bright and iridescent colours, while other dark ones fall down, far below, into a shadowy space.

Added to this is the massive division of society into innumerable castes and creeds, different languages, great distances between States and regions, some of which are really isolated, another reason for social inequalities to steadily increase. The problems of castes, which have resulted in a further stratification in society, based to begin with, on the varna (*colour*) of the skin, as castes are referred to in India, are also a factor. As much as Buddha and Gandhi wanted to eliminate them, one six centuries before Christ and another one in the 20th century, they could not! Bhimrao Ramji Ambedkar, the father of the modern Indian Constitution, was himself a pariah, and yet a jurist, academic and politician. He fought tirelessly for the rights of the Dalits, a caste to which he belonged. Many of whom converted massively to Buddhism, as this religion did not have the constraints that trap everyone born in India in a relentless social inertia. It is curious that Megasthenes, the Macedonian ambassador sent by Greece to the court of the Indian king Chandragupta Maurya (320–297 BC), made mention in his chronicle of a society that valued above all wisdom and honour, and in which there was a harmonious relationship between its castes, from the Brahmins to the peasants, passing through the warriors and artisans. Perhaps at that time it was a suitable model for a particular historical stage, but later, social mobility has been much slower as compared to elsewhere in the world.

This absorbing and blinding, although complex nation, works for now in a deeply contradictory and unbridled way. She does it as though like a brain that has a bright right hemisphere, endowed with an awakened intuition, from which haunting sounds and glittering images proceed, while the left hemisphere, that of the figures, that of the results, is incredibly tiny and stagnant. This, despite the great mathematicians that India has produced, the personal intuition of the rishis and yogis, who gave the concept of zero and many of the discoveries of contemporary physics and astronomy. The sphere of governance seems to be at odds with numbers! It is not logical nor does it foresee the serious situations that prevail! It hardly plans! And if it does, it does not get its calculations right. Except in the preparations for the parade on January 26, which begin months in advance, paralyzing the entire area of India Gate for a hundred days, for a morning of celebration, the Republic Day.

No one has been able to formulate what has been the true unifying element that has preserved India, and defines it as a people in the midst of this unlimited mosaic of a thousand faces. Nehru managed a country shocked after the Partition with Pakistan to get moving. Already at that time, in 1947, India had the germ of some industrial sectors, iron and steel, pharmaceutical, but concentrated in a few families: first, Tata, and after it Birla, Bajaj, Mittal, and others. The risks of it becoming a failed nation were colossal, because there were many elements against its formation, starting with the confrontation between the Hindu and Muslim communities, which caused hundreds of thousands of deaths and millions of exiles. Reformulating the territorial structure after the withdrawal of the privileges of the Maharajas and creating a new political and economic system, were just some of the internal challenges, in addition to other regional ones. The experiment can be said to have been successful on the whole, despite the thousand current difficulties, especially economic ones. It has been precisely the diversity of all kinds that has been the wealth and key to the salvation of the country, which should not be lost given the current ultra-nationalist governmental predilections.

In this complicated game of equilibria that occurred soon after independence, with a huge risk for the country, one of the most accurate measures taken by the founders of independent India was to create a federal state that would be, paradoxically strong and centralized. This allowed it to maintain a great religious, linguistic and cultural diversity, which did not tear it apart in the difficult national integration post-Independence. For this, the universal vote, carried out in the first free elections of 1951, based on a democratic system was fundamental, only suspended during the two years that the "state of emergency" (1975–1977) imposed by Indira Gandhi, lasted.

Until a few decades ago there was a great similarity in the widespread poverty among the population of China and India, with very similar figures in their per capita income. In 1960, China had $89 annually, and India practically the same, $83, while the difference today is 1,600 to 8,000. That is, Chinese personal wealth became more than four times higher.

There are, in fact, certain convergences between these two neighbouring giants, India and China, such as the very high population, and the boundlessness of the country, as also the enormous imbalance between the large cities and the rural areas of the interior. In spite of the mutual and recent rapprochement between both, a great distrust persists, mainly because of the border problems to the East and the West, as well as the proximity of Beijing to Islamabad in the nuclear field. One of the great differences in the present moment is that China ended sadly with a good part of its traditions and culture, as well as its religions gone, while in India these general and regional identities still have an undeniable strength, despite the fact that the violent eruption of the 21st century and technology, which instead of weakening, are actually enriching them. On the other hand, however, despite the economic opening that took place after the hard Communist Cultural Revolution, the secrecy and political immobility of the party, by definition the only one, persists in Beijing. This political element, is long-term a stabilizing element in favour of India, despite corruption and the many difficulties in leading a decent life for most of the population. The fact of having a settled democracy, in principle secular, despite its deep religious roots is to it's advantage.

Around these days came about the surprising case of a Sikh guru, Gurmeet Ram Rahim, sentenced to twenty years in prison for raping two girls 15 years earlier. Upon learning of the Haryana court's decision to convict him, his followers, numbering millions in Punjab and in several neighbouring states, mobilized in the most violent way, burning buses, and challenging law enforcement agencies, including in New Delhi. The result was 38 dead and innumerable wounded. This is not a guru after the kind of image that one usually has of them in the West, a recluse in meditation in his ashram. On the contrary, his appearance is that of a Demis Roussos of the 21st century, with the look of a gross rock star, who has starred in several films, and has something like fifty centres spread across north India.

This issue of false gurus, made me wonder… Is Indian spirituality a myth largely created and fostered by the West? Everyone is aware of the profound roots of Indian religions and mysticism, with their myriad manifestations in architecture, music, or philosophy, but the West has been responsible for this overestimation of Indian spirituality, over other more material approaches that have existed all along. One thing the West has certainly contributed to this "oriental" vision, is using it as a mere romantic getaway. The fact is that many of these false gurus, from Pune to Thanjavur, from Rajasthan to Maharashtra, have made use today of this very appeal of the famous "brand India". And they have done it with the most bizarre combinations of mysticism, blatant business and self-promotion in their ideas and suggestions. Contrary to what is expected of them, these experts of the late 20th and early 21st centuries, with their casual look, and cool social relations, have known how to present the problems of others to themselves. They are specialists in good-natured superficiality, apparent detachment, and above all, in their aversion to pain and anger, when obstacles and tests have always been necessary in the path to spiritual growth, in order to really transcend problems. They are subjects of easy words, and they move like fish in water in at least three languages, including, of course, English. Yes! The new gurus have really taken into account the signs of the times!

I would therefore like to assert that Indian spirituality is indeed a myth created throughout the nineteenth and twentieth centuries, largely by the West, but also comfortably exploited today by this country, especially in big cities. The brutal cocktail of materialism, with teachings "for the body and mind", causes great disappointment in those who come to spend some time, or to live in this land of the Vedas and of Buddhism. As a result of this, in recent decades, there have been several postmodern gurus... closer to fashion magazines, and the market than to traditional yoga or meditation. This subverts the master-disciple relationship that existed until a few decades ago, before the so-called "spiritual tourism" began. Hardly anyone in India bothers about the sadhus, who today appear dour and boring in the common imagination, something from the remote past. These are the times of a global clientele, of gurus who continue to address the masses, although now they do so especially for the rich and for the politicians. They promote a strange and explosive mixture of mysticism and declared materialism, whose effects are easy to predict. They do not have much more scope than the interests of each other. Gone are the vows of silence, chastity, or poverty, which makes the teaching qualitatively removed from the secular Indian spirituality, linked to the forests, the Himalayas and the long voluntary retreats. Nobody wants to talk about solitude, let alone resignation! To meditate is not to reflect, it is rather the opposite, it is about stopping the conscience, the inner dialogue.

Among those who started this difficult embrace of materialism with the world of yoga and spirituality, perhaps the best known was the "neo-tantra" movement of Bhagwan Rajneesh, later known as Osho. And he did it assaying impossible mixes, such as Zennis (fusion of Zen and tennis), which could as well be a joke, an iconoclastic irony. Someone said of him that he wanted to be Christ and Epicurus together, though he was rather the latter, roaming in the US with a large fleet of Rolls Royce. Such was the tragic end of his life, having to assume so many contradictions! They gradually distorted the original beginnings, until they atomized and disappeared.

In India, everything is extreme! From the master of highest asceticism, of Gandhian chastity, to the "guru of the rich", to the "sex guru", without intermediate steps. There would be nothing wrong in trying to achieve a supreme synthesis between the inner search and a comfortable life, even a very comfortable one—through the shared investment of one's own effort in spiritual energy, and in business. The problem is that given their obsessive nature, they hardly allow the required peace of mind, with which to combine meditation, and go deep into the self. The reason being that this is about different facets of the human being, which seek all energy to be dedicated exclusively to them, and one, almost always the same one, concludes by winning over the other. Spirituality is necessarily an invariable vital attitude, a way of life, it is not a set of ideas or beliefs that may change with the mood of the day, with the times…

Quite characteristic of this is the yoga in stadiums… Although one could also criticize opera in stadiums, which became fashionable in the West with the Three Tenors, and the argument of reaching out to macro-public. Always the macro! It's the times! We are facing a world without meaning, in which neither the East nor the West have a clear notion of transcendence. And unfortunately, many of those who contemplate it from that sacred side that every human being possesses, are fanaticized by group ideologies, or personal interests. Maybe, it cannot be otherwise in this day, with internet, and the speed with which one wants to print everything with the rapidity of information, with the constant novelty of the market, the competition at work, and with the neighbour. All of them together have ruined the self-discipline of the individual, rarely existing today with yoga and non-distorted meditation, concentration, patience, and all those concepts that seem to define India as against the West.

This, that someone has called "the spiritual acrobatics" of India could be compared with flamenco music for tourists in Spain. Heavy and repetitive music of very low quality, meant for foreign consumption, that is, for those who do not understand it, as against true flamenco for the connoisseurs. Therefore, perhaps to protect itself, true yoga, the genuine teaching of meditation, has been permanently hidden. The so-called progress and globalization have been devastating on a broad plane, because although yoga is present throughout the world, it is so almost like gymnastics, not as a spiritualization of body and matter, which is its origin, its meaning and its practice. Instead of delving deeper into the being, it is becoming more and more superficial.

Like all places that seemed privileged for a "quiet and meditative life", India has changed a lot in recent times. Its governments and part of its society have embraced the most extreme materialism, showing little compassion for those who suffer most from poverty. It seems an irreversible path, the one undertaken by this nation in the nineties of the last century, to be counted among the most powerful on Earth. But there is a very persistent reality—the social fabric does not accompany their desire for an "emerging nation", according to some already "emerged". I wonder what Gandhi would do today! Would he continue with his aversion to technology, his ultra -traditional vision, with its myth of rural past and virtuous poverty? It is very difficult to intuit! Perhaps he was more radical in his opposition to the modern world, and to technology as a substitute for all values.

One can observe curious phenomena in this field, such as when the guru in fashion offers himself through TV, in a stadium in the capital, before the masses, to be the master of the prime minister, perhaps seeing himself as a court counsellor! Such demonstrations made me think how far were the moments when, for example, Emperor Akbar interned into the woods to talk about the Upanishads with sadhus. How distant that seems! By contrast, modern gurus need to compulsively be seen from outside, like a third person who seeks admiration. And above all, senses that others need him! Like all those seeking social advancement and recognition, they usually have a stark inability to feel and love. What they require, definitely, is a narcissistic form of affection. And precisely because of this they succeed! Society itself augurs in them such eagerness! And that is also why they are so in accordance with the present times! This does not mean that they always have bad intentions, or lack knowledge of what they preach. It means that they need that kind of relationship with others. And they speak only of what they want to hear! They have a great appetite for popularity, which is fed back with the anonymous multitude of their disciples, a majority of them certainly. Very far from what we know as having experienced enlightenment, they are evidently those who are still dragging the heavy shadow of their "I" of their short biography. Many of them are not at all that luminous person who conveys a magical and privileged connection with the highest, as a guru one supposes would—an adult, transparent in the first place, and at the height of human development. On the contrary, many of those who call themselves gurus today are opaque, and even dark, not being able to move beyond their ego. In contrast, in a paradoxical and insatiable manner, they feed their *spiritual ego*.

INDIA

Capital of the Two Oceans

The real voyage of discovery consists not in seeking new landscapes, but in having new eyes.

Marcel Proust

Living in a city like New Delhi for a relatevely long period of time is never done easily or gratuitously. One can strive to achieve a successful installation from the first moment, give it all the enthusiasm and means, and persist, even when the difficulties of daily life, and the initial euphoria fades. But, no, you never manage to do it gratuitously! It seems like a universal objective, and almost a physical law, like water boiling at one hundred degrees, or freezing at zero. For some reason, a halo of extreme experiences surrounds India, particularly in the capital. A murky aura of contradictory and antagonistic elements meets here. It happens in the inexplicable proximity of opposites like the great maritime currents, the warm waters of the Gulf of Mexico, breaking through the cold Atlantic. Two very different temperatures that feed on circuits that are beyond our comprehension. Indeed, antithetical, disproportionate elements characterize the countryy as the beautiful and the horrible, the smelly and the fragrant, the heart-breaking and the restorative are all atomized, fused intimately with each other, like two half-brothers who need each other, even though they are apparently opposed in nature. It happens as with the primordial soup that physicists and astronomers talk about, after the Big Bang gave birth to the universe. That colossal explosion in which the nuclei of atoms had not yet been created, and its components teemed closely with the electrons at millions of degrees. Everything happened in a small inconceivably incandescent space, in which matter was yet pure energy, and where light had nowhere to be reflected, for it had still not separated from darkness.

Like that constant union of opposites, without distinctions, in the same space, another axiom that is learned here in the experiences of each one, is that India is either loved or hated! There is no indifference! I never saw anyone make a sceptical gesture or remark when the word "India" was mentioned. On the contrary, a serene smile, or a disapproving grimace are the only two known reactions. There is also a third possibility in the feelings that are held with respect to India! The matter of loving and detesting it intermittently, in alternating phases, like the swinging of a pendulum. Yes! This is not my extravagance or my genius! This circumstance is quite common, and without doubt, the closest to my experience. This eventual attraction or rejection, subject to cycles, to the events in the daily life of each one. It is not an ambiguity or lack of definition! It is a paradox in response to the Indian paradox itself! Even if you never really know how it works. For those who live or have lived in this land, the essential approach is in effect a kind of aphorism learned in their own skin, and found in the day to day life.

On this matter, and its daily unpredictable playing out, this feeling of being as though on a roller coaster, sometimes euphoric, at others despairing, I have concluded that there are at least three or four invisible lines. They are like strings of colours that are intertwined in our interior, and since they are hidden we cannot see them. It is these strings that together draw our mood, what happens outside, and all that happens within, from our health to the dreams that we have, good or bad, the weather at that particular time, all is recorded deep inside. When such lines converge at a point, a kind of activation occurs. It's like a crossing of particles, which occasions a great euphoria or a striking decay. Obviously, the same happens with this existential reckoning everywhere, but here it is far more extreme and variable.

It seems a cliché to say that New Delhi, or by extension India, can only be loved or hated, yet it is certainly what most often occurs. As in a good part of the rest of India, living in New Delhi is not simple, in fact, quite difficult to describe. Specially so if you want to break the routine established between home and work, specially if you want, more than anything else, to travel extensively, to the less touristy places throughout the country. But even in what one would consider a "standard" life of an expatriate, one suffers continuous conflicts of intendancy, unexpected bureaucratic hostility when making requests for permits and clearances, erroneous invoices, cheques returned for the most unexpected reasons, and visa renewals. The more we want to come and live here, the more will we be tested by India, the more will its "poison" be introduced between thin, microscopic interstices of our being, of our memories and desires, even our dreams, complicating our life limitlessly. As in ancient propitiatory rites of the goddess Kali, in which one had to appease the angry deity, if one wanted to stay here against all odds, one had to necessarily sacrifice something dear. It must be something that we find difficult to let go, and it means a kind of involuntary non-refundable donation. It is but from there the word sacrifice comes—a sacred trade. There is no other way out! Money, health and above all, time, an infinite time—months or maybe years to adapt to such a concrete and such an abstract identity as that of India.

After many years of New Delhi being the dusty and boring administrative capital of this immense country, almost forgotten and untended, compared to the glamorous and modern Bombay, or the modern and technologically advanced Bangalore, something undeniable moves and rouses today in its diverse neighbourhoods, like Hauz Khas, Greater Kailash, or Saket. Its protagonists are young people in particular, from the nascent national middle class, present already in many cities, although still not too visible in the face of the largely prevalent poverty in the streets. The new galleries and art venues of Lado Sarai, or music festivals and parks, are not alien to it. Nor are the very active cultural centres, such as the India Habitat Centre, and the innumerable five-star hotels scattered around the city, with a multitude of rooms, restaurants and events 365 days a year. This rebirth and new verve has also happened in a special way, in the commercial area of Connaught Place, which used to house the tailors and elegant establishments of the officials of the Raj, at the beginning of the newly inaugurated capital. A fabulous revitalization is taking place here, which radiates to the rest of the city with energy and determination. Innumerable bars on the upper floors, restaurants, both fast food and quality, have life that extends from the morning until late at night. It is surprising that not too long ago the well-to-do did not appear there, as it was seen as a marginal place with western backpackers on the move. Once the few and poorly stocked stores closed in the evenings, the place became the domain of stray and destitute dogs. But today things have changed! The new establishments have filled the arcades and corridors, bounded by elegant columns, with all kinds of merchandise. And they are likely to continue doing so!

In cities like Utrecht, or Venice, whose walls are constantly reflected in their narrow waterways, the gaze sometimes slides over them, over their surface, rather than on the buildings themselves. Other cities, like many Mediterranean, and Atlantic ones, have blue skies visible throughout their geography, thanks to their wide avenues or boardwalks, and make you always look upwards. New Delhi, however, is in neither of these two categories. Its skies, almost all through the year, appear opaque, ash-like, and tend to remain so throughout the day, contaminated by the fires lit at night, or by the dust in suspension, blowing in from the western desert. Thus, except for some fabulous sunsets, and some storms that create spectacular scenarios in the sky, the few times that something made me stare upwards were the big birds, the kites, and the crows in sweeping and sustained flights.

As with so many others, this is a city that is barely known beyond its surface. You have to possess both vivid historical and scholarly keys, in addition to walking around in it countless times, in the incessant bustle of its streets, its institutions, or markets, before hoping to acquire an appraised perception of it. Yes, I wanted to find the authentic keys of this city… such as the ones that when rotated, and introduced into appropriate points, open up mental spaces, with a perspective both current and historical. For such a difficult squaring the circle that I demanded of myself, I needed to identify the crucial places of New Delhi, across its endless monuments, corners, neighbourhoods, arteries, and points of particular significance, despite the endless annoyance of the neurotic traffic, and the discomfort of walking around in the hot weather that persists through most of the year…

It's about those special key sites and surfaces, like Connaught Place, or Nizamuddin, like Qutub Minar or the area around India Gate, the various spots of Old Delhi that never reveal their mystery, the meaning that is intuited, but escapes between the fingers… that is where one finds the essential axes, both of new and old Delhi. Nobody, except for a random tourist goes there to enjoy just walking around. Most pass by rushing, mechanically, almost like zombies, doing something very concrete—selling, buying or getting treatment. It is, therefore, a radical change of perspective, to discover spaces in the alleys opposite the old havelis, the dilapidated houses belonging to another era, inviting you to enter, with difficulty and not comfortably, through a skin of innumerable layers.

From the beginning I visualized this old and new capital, not as a whole, as something homogeneous and unified, as one generally does with most other big cities, but rather like islands, fragments floating in a waterless archipelago, without a recognizable centre. Between neighbourhood and neighbourhood, between colony and colony, in the immense space that New Delhi occupies, one feels like a true pilgrim travelling between distant and different "enclaves", on dusty asphalt, between satellites and cities impersonally founded by a blind destiny of unstoppable development. It is not really a city that can be perceived as a whole, but rather a conglomeration of zones, of sections, of diverse geographies, of families and castes, which nobody, absolutely nobody, of whatever social stratum or occupation, encompasses simultaneously.

New Delhi appeared to me as an immense labyrinth of multiple social, linguistic, religious, and cultural layers, to understand all of that I needed some keys that I still lacked. Yes, keys that open doors to spaces, to buildings and to the characters for their multiple entries and exits. Actually, this city is in itself a double labyrinth—the exterior and the interior, with a thousand isolated, disconnected circuits. So much so that I came to the conclusion, that each inhabitant has a Delhi that is his own and different from the rest. All this is largely the result of a brutal difference between public and private. Between the state enterprise and the private/commercial. Its infrastructure, services, communications, except the recent metro… are typical of a third world city—in the common spaces and in the streets, but the jump is meteoric if one turns towards the residences and the numerous luxury hotels.

The European perception ceaselessly notices the brutal clashes between the traditional world rooted in its ancestry, and the "globalized" contemporary world of the 21st century. The inhabitants, immersed as they are in the process, naturally do not see it that way. To them it is utterly "logical". It is true that it is inherent in human nature to live in extremes, to experience oneself in the counterpoint of experiences, loneliness and crowds, light and shadows, misery and excess, which no matter how much one tries, do not reconcile or get balanced. But in Delhi this is something that is taken to its final consequences. Something that is chewed and is breathed everywhere!

New Delhi is not only many cities in history, over time, eight, 8, 12, 21...it presently also includes many others, so it is not just neighbourhoods connected by roads that the city is made of. Saket has precious little in common with Vasant Vihar, or Chanakyapuri. In few places does one find the most miserable Third World sharing its space with the most extreme affluence, sharing the same space, but hardly touching each other, moving in distinct impermeable "closed circuits."

Yes, it can be asserted, without fear of taking sides, that New Delhi is a difficult city, which demands a lot and offers little in return. Or rather, She gives, in bits and pieces! She gives only when she wants to. Then she will lead you to the right place to reveal herself. Or she might never do it! She forces you to live in, or to pass through inhospitable and soulless places one day but the next day she could be kind, offering wide open windows with access to vistas you did not see before. Yes! When she wants, she reveals herself, without announcement, taking you by surprise. Here everything always happens like this, without warning, unexpectedly, lacking any continuity. Is it the light? Is it the environment? Is it the people who have two faces, one white and one black? Or is it the traveller?

At the beginning of the second year of my stay in this prodigious city, I got into the habit of going every Saturday morning to Old Delhi, or as it should be more properly referred to, Shahjahanabad, named after its founder, Shah Jahan, the great Mughal emperor, perhaps best known as the builder of the Taj Mahal, the magnificent mausoleum erected for his beloved wife Mumtaz Mahal, who died while delivering their fourteenth son. He was indeed, the last worthy representative of this dynasty, because although his son and jailer, Aurangzeb had made numerous military conquests in the south before his death, his fanaticism and narrow-mindedness in all areas, including social and cultural fields, led to an inexorable and profound decline after his long reign.

Every Saturday at 11 o'clock in the morning I would get picked up by the driver. After buying the inevitable croissants and other "Western" products that can only be found in Khan Market, we would head towards that congested area north of the city, which is opposite the red walls of the grand Fort. There I enjoyed an hour or two of walking through its streets, without direction or precise plans. In the central street of the Kinari Bazar, behind the North access road to the Great Mosque, there are numerous warehouses stacked with brass and copper objects, where you can find, sold by weight, an almost infinite number of idols of Hindu religion for worship, such as Ganeshas and Vishnus, also Buddhas, and some Tara figurines too. It is from here, then, that most emporia and stores selling such items receive their supplies, both in the capital as well as throughout the country. Because of my visits on numerous Saturdays, as a simple passer-by and not as a wholesale buyer, I developed a kind affability with some of the managers or shop owners. Since I was mainly interested in Buddhist art, we chatted quietly about whether a particular image of Buddha was in the Sarnath, Mathura, or Vihara style, or a Tara, Manjushri or Avalokiteshvara, or other bodhisattvas, were of Nepali, Indian/Ladakhi, or more rarely, of Tibetan origin. It should be noted that some of the owners of the most varied and interesting places were Sikhs. It is easy to recognize this from the names on the doors, with their unfailing surname—Singh: Man Singh, Jaspal Singh and others. I always thought on seeing the names how difficult it must be to distinguish between them when all the practitioners of this religion possess the noble and courageous surname of Singh, "Lion". The Sikhs know fairly well both Hinduism and Islam, being, at least in their origin, a kind of "middle way" between the two, although in habits and culture much closer to the first.

One of the most frequented shops belonged to an elderly man of delicate health. I wondered whether he was sick or worse, after seeing his establishment closed for a long time. Fortunately, it turned out that he was peacefully with his son in Canada, one of the countries, along with Australia and the US, where the Sikhs tend to emigrate the most. Another, let's say antiquarian, stuffed with Persian objects and copies of Mughal paintings, had, to my surprise, several pictures of King Juan Carlos on the wall of his shop, and although I did not understand the relationship very well, given the brief conversation because of the limited English, I gathered that one of his best clients, of many years ago, was a diplomat who worked in the Embassy of Spain! Another one hoarded a great variety of elephant bells, sold by weight. Yes, between the cauldrons and the brass figures, dulled or gleaming, sunken in the shade or flashing in the sunlight, these leisurely walks came late but were fruitful.

In fact, in Old Delhi there are only two or three antiquarians, or what we understand by the term in Europe, that is places where one can find and eventually buy more or less exotic and artistic objects at least one hundred years old. However, in that zone of access from the North to the Great Mosque, there are countless stores, or rather, warehouses, tiny or immense spread over several floors, where cult figures, in brass and bronze, such as Ganesha, Krishna, or Hanuman, among others, are sold at wholesale prices for both public and private temples. Sometimes, antique items also land up there, as though appearing from nowhere. One comes upon these stores as if by magic when one has been meandering along lanes lined by temples or houses. Some stores are visible because of their show cases, with some order in the display of objects for sale. Others are lost in alleys and inner courtyards, where one cannot reach if one is not escorted by someone who knows them. One of the most interesting and well stocked ones in that area is accessed by a narrow and steep staircase that would normally go unnoticed. Up there await wonders of stone and marble: Nandi (the bull of Shiva) of a dazzling white Makrana marble, pink stone Buddhas of Bihar: some imitations in black stone of Gandhara Buddhist art. And finally, Lakshmi, Krishna and Ganesha idols, intermingled without order or concert with Jain Thirthankaras, Vishnu, and other figures of worship. Some of them are real antiques from the grand houses or temples of South India and Gujarat but they called my attention much less.

What attracts me most in these objects found at random is that they show traces of life as it happened around them, imprinted in each and every one of their pores. Time, literally materialized in the accumulated dust in the grooves and cracks separates them from the chains of production of standardized forms found in other places. It particularizes them with a breath of their own! Some of these objects seem in fact to breathe, to be waiting for us since an eternity in a dark corner. We detect them in the distance, and we hear them speak, but not with articulated sounds, with long tirades, but as whiffs of breath, with a charge that electrifies only those who are attracted to them, and leaves the rest indifferent, with the slowed heartbeat of an animal for a long time, asleep. In no case do they do it with ordinary phrases, but with closed esoteric words that must be interpreted after a prolonged exercise, and on many occasions after a fascinating immersion. Then we hear them calling on us to get them back to life!

Something must remain in me of that hunter-gatherer instinct that since the dawn of time we carry inside, which in no way can be satisfied by supermarkets, or department stores—always uniform and predictable, where you can hardly make discoveries. In my case, I seem to continue with an unfulfilled thirst for everything that is there by chance, a thirst that I want to satisfy in antique shops and curios, albeit in a naïve though eventually effective manner. If such a need, and such a feeling, did not continue in some way to live among certain people, including in myself, given that we no longer hunt, materially, in order to eat, these outings, impelled by something unknown, would not make sense.

One who ventures through Chawri Bazar, which paradoxically means "the big meeting place" despite its narrowness, behind the Grand Mosque (Jama Masjid), discovers an endless amalgam of rickshaws, porters, and over the heads of all of them, tangled electric wires that crisscross the space above and across the street. Miraculously they bring light to the hundreds of microscopic wholesale stores dealing in reams and rolls of paper. It is hard to cross over to the other side just a few meters away because there is no space between wheel and wheel for one to put one's foot down in order to move forward. Anyone who strolls like an observer, will be constantly pushed by individuals who rush at him at full speed, brushing past or colliding with him, without apologizing. In this wholesale paper market you can find all kinds of paper—handmade, glazed, unprocessed, printed, colourful for gift wrapping and for decorating. But what it is really packed with, and what reigns over the rest, are the shops where you choose and order wedding cards. In their tiny windows, and inside their dark interiors, there is an infinite number of forms, letterheads, cards in colours and designs suited to all religious communities in Delhi, but mostly for the Hindu majority. Beyond the simple card paper invite that announces the betrothal and the time and place of the happy event, in recent times the fashion of inviting with something more voluminous has been imposed, a box, sometimes of large dimensions, which can have within it, anything from nuts to small jewellery, candy boxes, and more.

Despite the strong smells, the dust and dirt, I found great pleasure in merely wandering through the alleys of Old Delhi. Having to dodge the motorbikes which brush past the poor pedestrian at a speed that seems they are going to extinguish a fire, did not prevent me from heading, every Saturday towards the rear of Jama Masjid, the Great Mosque of the Mughals. After buying "by weight" a motley collection of books, sold in Darya Ganj, an extremely busy intersection between the new and the old city, the driver would drop me there and wait in the car for me at Meena Bazar, facing the ramparts of the Red Fort. I always began my customary walk from Dariba Kalan, the silver street, where I never really bought anything, to enter Kinari Bazar, the paper souk, passing through the bazar for brass and bronze objects and religious figures, which certainly was the one that attracted me the most, the one I enjoyed most. The real core of my walk! Most times I did not leave from there with arms and hands empty, and I gradually built up a collection of Buddhas, Taras, Maitreyas, Manjushris, and other bodhisattvas, both old and of current foundry, figurines that little by little, without my intending to do so, filled a good part of my house in Sundar Nagar. As is known, in the Buddhist Mahayana conception, present in northern India, Tibet and Japan and also elsewhere in Asia, the bodhisattvas are those beings who upon illumination, remain at the edge of definitively leaving the chain of reincarnations, in order to help the rest of humanity to "cross" the tribulations of existence. Beyond this, on the other side, is what every Hindu, Jain or Buddhist aspires to reach—moksha, nirvana—the final termination, a release from having to return to live in the dense world, a world fundamentally loaded with matter, where pure consciousness hardly finds a place to reveal to each being, its true nature. The void!

Sometimes, if I still had time and wanted to continue walking, I would head towards the very busy Chandni Chowk, where I almost always spent a few moments at the Jain temple by the corner, Shri Digambar Jain Lal Mandir, and also entered, a little beyond, into the Gurdwara Sis Ganj Sahib. I generally stayed there for a good while shielded from outside noise, listening to the recitation of the Guru Granth Sahib, the holy book of the Sikhs, which is considered a living guru. I enjoyed the music accompanying the recitations of this open, syncretic and inclusive religion, which at the same time was so close to Hinduism, and loaded with an intense unitary and indivisible perception of divinity.

It didn't make sense to go to Old Delhi on weekdays because the stores where one would find anything worthwhile are closed, and you only find trinkets, synthetic clothes, and simple elements of subsistence being sold on the sidewalks. Also I never went before noon, because the few places I was interested in, antique dealers and merchants dealing in leather goods, opened their shops around that time, and I usually stayed there till well into the afternoon. Another reason I did not visit the area during the week is because I was always busy in the studio, and in the work in Chanakyapuri, finishing the construction of the house that had brought me to India. That was something that I felt happy about almost every day—the fact of being here. And this in spite of being so far from home, with so many airplane hours involved, in addition to the daunting task of managing, every day, life that sometimes became unexpectedly complicated in the smallest of matters, those that in other places would get resolved automatically.

Sometimes, on a Sunday, when upon leaving home, alone, or with a visitor from Spain, I would go without hesitation to the Red Fort, since it was the only interesting place open in the whole city, in addition to the National Archaeological Museum. The museum was a place apart, a mine of constant discoveries in the halls of sculptures, both of bronze and stone, plus delicious Mughal miniatures, which open in their small format, an entire world. The first time I entered the Red Fort, beyond that huge red wall which seems to shelter lives from another time, it reminded me vividly of the Topkapi Palace in Istanbul. The public part, near the entrance, and the private, interior one, which looks at the old riverbed of the Yamuna, are adjacent, and although well defined, they barely have any thresholds marking the change. Rather, they are separated by lines, by walls. I also recognized many Ottoman elements in the architectural order, and the style of the ornaments—the cypress, the cream like white chiseled marble of the great columns. All those details reminded me, like the water, the chrysanthemums and the small waterfalls or *shellal*, in Arabic, designed on white marble and stone to cool the air in the stifling days of a long Delhi summer. What breathes in the private areas is the aspiration to paradise…the Islamic ideal of every garden, symbolized by the mere presence of water.

During the morning walks through the Lodi Gardens, the crows made me stop by always calling my attention, both by their easy and elegant gliding flight, as well as their hopping movements on the ground. I would look at them closely, cramming near the fountains to drink water, or splashing in the waterlogged lawns preening, circling, showing an enormous grace and curiosity about everything. It is therefore striking that in almost all geographies the crow has always been associated with bad luck. Why in the legends and mythological tales from around the world have these quotidian birds been held as sinister beings, associated with the unknown and the tenebrosity of the beyond? Observing them, and following the latest scientific research on them would tell us that they are intelligent creatures with a sense of "humour," who like playfulness and social relations.

The ability of these birds to imitate the sounds of the surroundings and "vocalize" them is also surprising. Like many other living beings, not only the winged, they can imitate in their own register, for example, the barking of dogs. The crows devise strategies, like throwing berries and nuts so that pedestrians or cars, break them as they pass over them, and thus enable the birds to eat them. According to researches carried out, they even seem to be aware of themselves and recognize themselves in the mirror. Likewise, these corvids are able to solve certain spatial problems, and do themselves proud in various laboratory experiments, which only animals of privileged intelligence, such as apes, elephants, or dolphins, are capable of solving. However, it is true that if they find a sick or dead congener, or if a chick falls out of the nest, they have no qualms about eating it.

Crows inhabit almost the whole planet, and as other big birds, they are usually in pairs. Only young individuals live alone. Eggs are greenish, with brown spots, and usually laid in a clutch of five. Also, parents feed the babies, for whom they show great affection, with insects, worms and small mice, or droppings from other animals.

In northern Europe specially, the crow has had great importance in mythology. According to the Germanic legends the god Odin is accompanied by two ravens, Hugin and Mugin, who he sends out to fly over the Earth and report to him everything they see in it. Odin himself was also known as the Raven God, and his own daughters, the beautiful Valkyries, would transform into ravens to collect the souls of dead warriors in a battle, and take them to their paradise, Valhalla.

In fact, the crow is not necessarily linked to evil, but rather to the occult and the mysterious, and participates as a privileged totemic animal in very different shamanic rituals throughout the world. Crows confer special insight and knowledge on all rites. They are able to communicate omens, and in all these cultures, both Eastern and Western, they are found close to the terrain of death while possessing the faculty of transporting souls. The vision that was imposed, specially in Christianity, with their negative representation in the Bible, is that crows are related to witchcraft and the devil, they are loaded with evil and are carriers of evil omens. With his shiny black feathers, the raven was seen as the antithesis of the White Dove, as a carrion bird who became bearer of death, pestilence and war.

Close to my studio, which had already become my regular work space, I was always struck, as I went by, by a privileged place that gave the appearance of providing great tranquility—an unusual garden, located between the bustling maelstrom of Jan Path and Parliament Street. When I was going or returning through the area, a little beyond the Imperial Hotel, it would appear every day, without my looking for it, like a haven of peace, like a breath of fresh breeze that seemed to come from another time, from another planet. It was not exactly from the past that it came, not from something finished, but from something as open as all that belongs to the future is. This place was the astronomical observatory of Jantar Mantar, today converted into a park, entry to which is on the payment of a small fee. The young specially frequent it, sitting on the grass there, which in a way challenges the concrete and the asphalt, as well as the noise and pollution caused by the innumerable buses that during all hours of the day circumambulate it ceaselessly. It is one of the five astronomical observatories built in India by the Maharaja of Jaipur, Jai Singh, a great fan of Astronomy and the Sciences, contemporary with the Age of Enlightenment in Europe. The first and perhaps the model for the others is the Jantar Mantar at Jaipur, located in the complex of the royal palace in the Pink City. The second one is the one in New Delhi. The others are in Ujjain and Benares. The fourth one in Mathura, no longer exists.

This fabulous Jantar Mantar of New Delhi was built in 1724, on lands that the Maharaja's family acquired through matrimonial alliances with the Mughals, and which were later given for free to the British, to erect the "new Rome" of the East. This observatory was about ten kilometres to the south, on the outskirts of the city raised by the fifth Mughal emperor, Shah Jahan, the city of Shahjahanabad, perhaps as a portent, a sign of the place where New Delhi would spread out two centuries later. The capital of the British Empire from 1911, New Delhi was called upon to replace the former capital of the Mughal empire. These two, along with the Empire of Ashoka, centred in Pataliputra, being the three moments of expansive imperial power in the millennial history of India.

Ever since I visited this place, the first time by chance, shortly after arriving in the city, it awakened my imagination and kindled my interest in the most vivid, almost constant manner, demanding of me to know more and more about it, its origin, its applications, and its history. Each time I walked or drove past its fences, I could not stop thinking about the strange scientific devices that were there, truly extravagant, "utopian", constructions, which connect little to the profane and the mundane but serve to know many "secrets" of the cosmos, the climate, the annual calendar, and the hours… Fallen into ruin, the Jantar Mantar was fortunately restored in part in the mid-19th century, after the visit of the German soldier and scientist Leopold von Orlich. Finally, in 1910, Maharaja Sawai Madho Singh II commissioned Pandit Gokal Chand Bhavan, descendant of the first builder of the observatory, to restore these four privileged enclaves existing in the country. The work was carried out between 1901 and 1923. During such restorations some changes were undertaken, such as introducing clocks with western time system, based on hours, minutes, and seconds, replacing the traditional Indian time scales method. He also built a new sundial on the so-called Samrat Yantra, on top of a pillar that already existed.

As the cities became bigger and bigger, densely populated and heavily polluted, the astronomical observatories had to be necessarily moved out. That happened in the early 20th century, with the instauration of electric light. These observatories began to be moved to clear and uninhabited places, such as islands and deserts, or preferably elevated places.

Jai Singh was an astrologer and a poet, two interests that usually do not meet together, even though the word seeks to transcend language, revealing presence, and cosmography tries to unravel what lies beyond man. The cosmos, the stars have much to do with the night, with the infinite shadow in which every appearance is possible. It has to do with restoring unity with the near and the distant. In that sense, it has to do with the link between the macro and micro cosmos.

Though visible from outside throughout the day, at the end of the afternoon, hidden in the middle of the heat and dust of the traffic that surrounds it, Jantar Mantar would reveal itself as a place as attractive as it was hermetic or secluded. For one wanting to flee from the hellish traffic, it beckons one to enter and to stay a good while, enjoying the freshness of the grass. But once inside, one must be prepared to accept a rhythm very different from the one that prevails outside! The steps, as one walks become slower and more rhythmic, and the vague presence of the cosmos on these lawns imposes thoughts different from those that exist outside. It is a real pity that this magnificent and astonishing enclave, this small park next to Connaught Place, is not open at night. I can testify that many times I have noted the fall of light and the rise of the moon create a special scenery there, which even from outside makes it extremely mysterious and enchanting. So much so, that on more than one occasion when I saw a splendid sky with a full moon, I felt a real temptation to jump the fence, enter the garden, lie on its freshly cut grass, in the centre of the Ram Yantra—that double circular building, which used to calculate the altitude of the sun and the stars. The stars! Those that today can hardly ever be seen in the sky, obscured and violated by smoke and light. Only occasionally, between October and March, does one get to glimpse of Venus, as a special privilege, and enjoy beautiful sunsets, with a huge red sun, followed by an enigmatic orange moon.

This space vividly reminded me of the world of European "utopian" architects of the 18th century, with the French Étienne-Louis Boullée (1728–1799) at the head. He believed that architecture is not only the art of building, but, and above all, of thinking. Think not through stark concepts, naked ideas, but through images, volumes, lights and shadows, textures and geometric patterns. His most famous works, such as the project for the cenotaph of Newton, could never be built, perhaps because they were unrealizable at that time. And they seem to belong in a clear way to the future, with respect to any time. They do not seem to be of the 18th century as the same time the Jantar Mantar was built. Boullée clearly differentiated between architecture and construction. While the first is for him creative inspiration, the second is reduced to an almost mechanical knowledge, repetitive and inert. Like Ledoux, the other great French "utopian" creator, Boullée took architecture for total art, and even as they were into the ideal, they also worked to solve urban and social issues, that would later emerge to the surface in the nineteenth and twentieth centuries. For Boullée, the most perfect form could not be anything other than the sphere. He thereby eliminated all unnecessary ornamentation. He hardly used anything other than geometric shapes like cubes, cylinders, pyramids, among others, always concentrating on the play of light and shadows. He was the great innovator in the use of this polarity of light, and influenced contemporary architects like Aldo Rossi.

The Jantar Mantar observatory is part of the Ptolemaic tradition, shared by many civilizations, including Islamic Iranian, within which the Zich astronomical tables were developed. This book, compiled by the Persian astronomer Nasir Al-Din Al-Tusi very precisely tabulates the parameters used for the calculation of the movement and position of the moon, the sun, the planets, and the stars. He proposed the most advanced planetary system of his time, and one of the most used until the arrival of the heliocentric paradigm. He carried out his work in the famous observatory of Maragha which was completed in 1259, and is located in the east of Azerbaijan, established under the patronage of Hulagu Khan, grandson of Genghis Khan and ruler of that Khanate in the 13th century. The Maragha observatory occupies an absolutely unique place in the history of medieval astronomy, since it was the model for all those that were built in this part of the world for several centuries, and their annotations of the movement of the stars transcended their borders to influence the Copernican revolution.

The instruments of the Jantar Mantar impress due to their enormous dimensions for the time, but also for their seemingly capricious forms. The first thing we come across is an equinoctial sundial, known as Samrat Yantra. It has that name for being dedicated to Pandit Jagan Nath, preceptor and then adviser to Jai Singh, when he was awarded the title of Samrat (emperor) for his outstanding knowledge and work in astronomy. This structure is used to calculate the solar time through the sun's culmination on the meridian, and the duration of day and night. It has curved stairs to the right and left, and in the centre in the NS direction, a very high straight staircase on a large right-angled triangle that seems headed towards the heavens, as if—touching the skies, it would end up in the void. Employed since ancient times, sundials are instruments to measure the passage of time by the rotation of the great star during the day. They use the shadow projected by the gnomon, a kind of bar that casts a shadow on a surface marked with a scale, to measure the apparent solar time. It made me think of Mesopotamia, of the Achaz Quadrant, an 8th century BC sundial, and how the passage of time was calculated by the shadow of the sun falling on the steps of the ziggurat. All this was something that really struck me from the beginning. The whole of this place is in good part, based on the play of light and shadow. I was fascinated by the projection of the sky on Earth, with the delicate but effective mediation of man to work his calculations.

Another instrument that strongly attracted my attention was the Niyat Chakra Yantra, which served to establish the periodicity of celestial phenomena, periodic cycles, as well as the lunar and solar calendar. Equipped with surrounding and internal stairs, it looks like a female vulva, with its internal and external lips, or, like an open heart.

At the end of the park is the impressive Ram Yantra named after Maharaja Ram Singh, an ancestor of Sawai Jai Singh. It is composed of two high, hollow, circular walls, almost 8 mts in diameter, with the floor divided into thirty spaces. This instrument is used to determine the altitude and the azimuth of the sun, thanks to the shadow of the central pillar. At dawn, its shadow falls on the upper edge, which indicates that the solar altitude is 0, while the altitude of the sun is maximum at local noon, when the shadow of the pillar is shorter.

Although looking up to the universe, I also felt something under the feet, like a navel of the earth. In these special places there seems to emerge from the entrails of the earth an energy undoubtedly beneficial to our health and wellbeing. I was always fascinated by the first observatories, even the prehistoric ones, those moments in which man looks at the sky to try to know more about the immensity that surrounds him, not only to find answers to what can affect him, but as though anticipating that one day he would travel there. An unfathomable perplexing environment surrounds these miradors, these observatories, opening towards the mysteries of the cosmos. They have something seemingly outside time and space, that unites man with the cosmos, thanks to the physical and metaphorical power of their devices. As a highly evolved Stonehenge, in the first astronomical observatories, observation came more from an intuitive, experiential approach to the stars, to know the solstices and equinoxes.

Everything arises from the initial admiration of man as he gazes at the celestial bodies to detect and follow them, something that goes back to the night of human times. Over time, his impulse would end up nurturing mythology and religion in his observation of astral movements, and later, science. How not to think, for example, of the caves of Lascaux, in France? They have in their cave paintings (17,000 BC) the representation of a true star map, with the Constellation of Taurus, and the Pleiades.

Here one is dealing with another logic, different from the Aristotelian logic in which we Westerners are immersed, and which has trained us in the "principle of non-contradiction", according to which Black cannot be white at the same time. Here in everyday life, two things are not exclusive of each other, to begin with, because they happen to be contrary. Here, something can be itself and its opposite at the same time, and without explanation.

I cannot forget that occasion, when we halted at a traffic light close to home, at the confluence of two major arterial roads—Subramania Bharti Marg and Zakir Hussain Marg. We had been stuck for a long time on my usual route to work. Even though I knew very well how long this traffic light took to change, there came a moment when the long wait started seeming strange to me since it was apparent that we were not held up because of VIP movement or anything like that. It was then that I saw to my left, a young policeman under a leafy tree, seated before the box of controls that regulated the traffic lights at the intersection. The man was manipulating the keys, as I had seen many times before, maybe because the system was stalled, or someone special was going to pass by that road.

However this time was different from other desperate waits—the man was in the midst of a very animated conversation on his mobile phone in his right hand, but had forgotten to press the controls to change the direction of the flow with his left hand. It seemed of little consequence to him whether others moved on or not! And so the time passed, while he gesticulated and laughed with whoever he was talking to—a friend, or wife. What was evident was that it was not about work, or anything to do with traffic. He just did not remember to use his left hand to direct us onward for a full quarter of an hour. Once again I noted that the long-suffering drivers of the high officials and embassies, especially in this residential area, are accustomed to long waits at the roundabouts and confluences of the streets, due to the presence of official convoys. Hardly anyone honked to interrupt the policeman's animated chatter. Finally, with a smile on his face—as if nothing had happened, he pressed the appropriate key. And we were able to move! Nothing had happened there apparently! Well, time does not count!

As a result of a meeting with some structural technicians in the studio, one day I was invited to visit the Department of Architecture of Symbiosis University, a prestigious private institution in the city of Pune. I suppose that like many other privileged universities, it is conceived of, not only for Indian students, but also for the children of the elites from those anglophone countries like Afghanistan, Yemen and many others in Africa and Asia, where it is barely possible to get quality education with minimal disruption. On my arrival in this city of western India, modern, at the same time historic, and largely dedicated to teaching and technology, two young professors picked me up from my hotel in the city centre to drive me to the campus, on the outskirts of the city. Once there, I was taken on a tour of the Department of Architecture and Arts. We began with the departments of Drawing, of Composition, then went on to those of Projects, of Territorial Planning, and Urban Planning, which I hope will some day be applied in India, where we see satellite cities coming up without any planning, and raised without any functionality. They also took me around the campus, surrounded by somewhat arid hills, perhaps because of the time of the year, to visit other departments, such as the Mass Communications one, and others. Although I am not a specialist in this area, I think they had the best sets, armed with the latest cameras and equipment. And we also saw, not far from there, the sports facilities.

A little later, after some refreshments, we went back to the starting point. I noticed next to the Vice-Chancellor's Office there was an impeccably maintained helipad, the first private one I saw in India.

As a reflection and one of the consequences of that instructive visit, I realized then, on my way back to Delhi, that India is by no means a single unit. "An" India!. I do not mean in the political sense, which obviously it is, but in the experiential sense. When living and travelling through it, one perceives it as an indefinite series of bubbles, of different colours, floating in an inexhaustible diversity. Within them, one has such different experiences that they do not seem to correspond to one single place, and make that phrase "Anything that can be said about India is true, as much as its opposite", ring true. I was thinking, indeed, in addition to the huge differences of levels between one state and another, between one city and another, are the brutal gaps that exist in the country, especially between the private and the state sector. It seems an incontestable reality that creativity and growth is largely in private hands—a situation that is not likely to change in a long time! The centralized State, a common administration for the whole country, except in Defence, Foreign Relations, and Business, is barely tangible, except when it comes to adopting populist measures with elections in the vicinity. In the day to day life of the many millions of citizens, little is really done to facilitate their existence with essential improvements in health, communications, or education. Not only are there as many Indias as cities or neighbourhoods, there are as many as there are universities, and hospitals. Such is the distance and the difference between the planners and that which is lived in the street!

Old and New Delhi are two cities with their backs turned to each other! They function as two hearts of the same body, though with different beats, out of sync and disparate. It even seems likely that from this strange relationship between the two would emerge, in a difficult pirouette, in a mortal triple somersault in time, a third Delhi. Yes, a New New Delhi, although this time not fused into something recognizable, as we understand a city to be, with roots and recognizable faces, but dispersed, without any identifiable image. Gurgaon, Noida, and Saket are these satellite cities, or cluster neighbourhoods. How to classify them? As a soulless body, they arise simultaneously, specially in the south, growing like foam. They have come up as a response to the need of an expanding young population, but without any planning. A kind of cold and distant experiment for an unpredictable future. They do not have urbanism nor any of the characteristic constructions that cities hitherto had such as a recognizable centre, parks or monuments, buildings for civic administration. They have nothing of all that! They can hardly, therefore, have a soul, or breathe, being a jumble of roads and concrete, an aggregate of immense buildings, between flyovers and asphalt seas, where a human being cannot walk and will never find his place. People do not find spaces there in which to walk around like in most cities, and cannot maintain a simple conversation with neighbours or friends. If this is the future proposed for the cities, like the one which appear in science fiction films, where you cannot walk, and everything is just immense masses of metal. Let's run away from it!

"There is nothing worth while, when one is already in Old Delhi!" I said to my wife in a moment of outburst, in one of the worst situations that I had to live through in the farm house during those hard times at the beginning of my stay. Put simply, my initial enthusiasm for the city, both old and new, for its fascinating "islands", gardens, bazars and monuments, had been drastically dimmed, tinging with black everything, without exception, of the rest of the landscape. I could talk only about my problems due to insomnia, which had robbed me of much of my work and the rest of my life during those initial months. Months of initiation into what, I still do not know!

Although I knew the Red Fort superficially, its gardens and pavilions in the interior, the gates of the fortress, and the entrance bazar, next to the bazar of Old Delhi, in those early days of my arrival, they did not attract me at all. All interest in moving beyond Jantar Mantar and Connaught Place had vanished, as also the desire to explore the north of the city, built by the British, at least until the project of the house was channelled and my life settled. Fortunately, once I left the farmhouse, and with a "new life" inaugurated in the colony of Sundar Nagar, the lens of my conscience, and with it my daily life, finally opened up and relaxed. It also opened up the map of my imagination and my interest in visiting that area towards the north of the capital. What a joy! What a blessing to be able to walk relaxed and carefree through the bazars! What a pleasure to make my way among the chaos of vehicles and people without experiencing regret, and feeling serene! Although it was already May, and the next is the worst month of the year, due to extreme heat and dryness, it did not matter! I could finally take a deep breath and see things clearly!

After getting rid of the nightmare of insomnia, I could concentrate on putting my own house in order, with furniture newly arrived from Spain. This distinctive house, in the comfortable colony of Sundar Nagar built shortly after independence by affluent Indian families, lay between Purana Qila and Humayun's Tomb. Like other residential enclaves in New Delhi, it is curious that this locality did not have a single grocery store, but boasted of several jewellery and antique shops, perhaps the only ones worth the name in the city. This colony, maybe together with Golf Links and Jor Bagh, considered the best in the capital, has a homogeneous appearance, discreetly elegant and relaxed in its architecture, very green in its layout. This means that the temperature here is at least two degrees lower than in the rest of the city, which in summer is vital, and makes you sleep better than anywhere else. In a style close to the Bauhaus of the 1930s most of the houses are still in their original condition—with two large floors, and a front garden, followed by a patio, and in the back, a garage and accommodation for the servants.

I already had in there all the clothes, books, folders of drawings, and the thousand objects that I needed for my daily life. Things began to regain meaning! The names of the places and the people that for a while had evaporated from my mind, and had remained in limbo as a result of stress, came back again. After the involuntary halt, the neurons started up in places as deep as decisive in my brain. Again I could link the concepts with clarity, articulate images cleanly in my mind, until recently the abilities which were dulled by the obsession to change my inverted sleep pattern.

Like New York, New Zealand, or New South Wales, all places starting with New were created during the colonial conquests between the seventeenth and nineteenth centuries, thousands of kilometres away from European civilizational centres that gave them the name. The case of Mughal Shahjahanabad, the capital before the British New Delhi, is quite different, because although both cities are quite the opposite of each other, they also meet when you say just Delhi, melting into each other without cuts or transitions, when not specified whether Old or New. The old city is a tangle of narrow streets and asphyxiating alleys, without a single tree, where it is almost impossible to move around in a vehicle. The New, on the contrary, has a huge network of straight avenues, without a single curve, which at certain hours are completely deserted. This New Delhi of grand walkways with trees and bungalows with generous gardens, represents the city of the select, of high officials and diplomats, as well as of privileged owners of big mansions, inhabitants of that New Rome, as described by George V during the founding ceremony of the city in 1911. On the contrary, the old city is a frantic anthill with millimetred spaces for each being, where nothing rests, round the clock and it is difficult to breathe during much of the year. Like a magnet, however, it possesses a rare appeal that despite its dusty and decrepit appearance, makes it work with intensity for those who come to it.

To a certain extent, both complement each other in their contradictions. The presence or absence of the past is something that also clearly distinguishes both the cities. As against the numerous temples and mosques of the old city, and the monumental doors, like Kashmiri Gate or Delhi Gate, which lie forgotten between the crazy traffic, the new city, except for a tomb or two from the Mughal era, or that of the Sultanate, scattered around Golf Links, the area of Lodi, and Nizamuddin, this New Delhi is a city with hardly any memory of anything past. My most usual walks used to be in Lodi Park, and less often in the green areas stretching from the India Gate to the Presidential Palace, as well as in Jantar Mantar or some other rare "island" of peace in the city.

Despite the hundreds of thousands, maybe the millions of people who walk the streets of New Delhi every day, it is curious that there are no simple strollers. Or if there are, it is despite themselves. Most of them are going on some errand, concerning their work or their family. They usually go at full speed, thinking, step after step during their march, of the countless problems that daily life presents to them. At the other end of the social extreme, for anyone from the ascending "middle class", not to mention the new rich, walking seems old, third world-ish, a step backwards, more for the poor, the needy, those who have not joined the "new India". Nobody from the so-called upper "middle class", being able to go comfortably by car with air conditioning, always with air conditioning and the windows raised, will descend to the level of the wheels, will go down to the unpredictable streets, to the rare and rugged sidewalks, fighting for the limited space with the destitute and the deprived. The only leisurely passers-by of New Delhi are found in certain parks like the Lodi Garden, Siri Fort, Nehru Park, and some around Civil Lines. In such places one can see people walking, in tracksuits or comfortable clothes, couples of all ages, groups of especially older people, who, because of diabetes, high blood pressure or other diseases, mild or severe, have been advised to walk and breathe "pure" air at a certain time of the day. In such cases, they make it clear, by the choice of place and the clothes they wear, that it is a sport, a voluntary physical exercise, and in no way an obligation.

However, something unites them all, the walkers both voluntary and forced. From the poorest to the wealthiest, whatever be the social and economic class they belong to, they have one thing in common. They all march in a hurry to do something! And they make it clear that they are in a hurry! No wasting time with long, hesitant steps, or a reflective attitude. Even the needy, it seems, walk looking for specific things. No one is in the habit of taking an "open" walk for the pleasure of strolling, observing from a distance what one finds on the way, even if it is only to de-automatize one's life, to contemplate everyday problems with another attitude and a different perspective—as a Buddhist would say: without seeking the fruits of their action. No doubt that in the villages and in the rural world the situation is different. There are more contemplative and relaxed attitudes, typical of ancient India, the India of always. But in large cities, and the modern satellite population, it is definitely speed, competitiveness as a life attitude which has triumphed. It is something from which there is no turning back, and that generates the vicious cycle of constant stress. Sometimes, all this seems to generate a remarkable euphoria, a cerebral over-excitement, especially in the so-called "emerging" classes, given over to consumerism, who, after the excitement of the purchase, and the closed deals, once back home, experience a big slump, even despondency.

For some this great city is pleasant, even exciting, while for others New Delhi is odious, impracticable, intestine-like in its twists and turns with no way out. The truth is that the city has a layered history and becomes an accomplice of those who try to rediscover its background. Not the banalities of easy relationships or the picaresque, but of the deep interconnections between its historical zones and their environmental elements. This however, requires knowledge and patience! For those who approach it with determination and perseverance, and alertness, it reveals its secrets. Even though it appears to be a difficult and ungrateful city, with many spikes and edges, New Delhi often reserves sights which are difficult to ignore! These can be found in the soft fog of winter, when Rashtrapati Bhavan and India Gate, at either end of the grand avenue, Raj Path, seem to levitate. Also, sometimes you can enjoy sunsets with huge red suns, and you feel they will remain forever up there, without dropping down below the horizon.

Few cities reveal themselves in a first visit. Often a more relaxed penetration is necessary! And New Delhi is no exception! But it is one of those that make you wait the longest! In my case, an already seasoned walker came to her to build a large house, with a large cluster of images and memories, formed by what he had seen around him in countless other cities. For such a stroller those places were a living and open book, which he'd left open in the memory to reinterpret from time to time. To me, an experienced walker is someone who does not allow himself to hurry after anything, or after anyone. He appears slow in his steps perhaps, but he is quick with the gaze, as also with his imagination and his mute but active memories, which make him analyze spontaneously—all that surrounds him. Actually, such a walker acts as a great reader who converts cities into huge books, in large collages composed of a thousand adhering elements, both material and intangible, both sordid and sublime. He explores its streets, its short or long history, its often imperceptible changes of ambient light, extracting meanings, marvelling at the multiple reality of the quotidian that appears to be waiting to be deciphered by him, as though confiding in him at that precise moment. All the signs are legible, and he goes after them in changing or repeated itineraries, by car or on foot. Even the most ordinary day can end up being a dazzling discovery in New Delhi due to its streets, squares, alleys, small craft workshops, mosques, as well as all kinds of temples—Hindu, Jain, Sikh. All of them possess a presence and a voice with a deep echo that never fades away!

Such a stroller is kind of one urban nomad! He is selective and respectful with everyone, but feels no obligation to do anything with anyone. He is a kind of "deluxe" exile, who despite being well anchored in his perceptions and reflections, in the eyes of the locals, seems to float, uncommitted to anything or anyone. Attentive and aware, this anonymous, foreign pedestrian does not, however, stop observing or participating in his own way, with his imagination, with his resources, in what is happening around him. He wanders, but he does so in a contemplative way, without considering himself more or less than anyone! The supreme right of such a walker, which ought always to be reserved, depends on whether he is interested in what he comes across, or prefers to pass it by.

Even if seemingly passive, the vocation of this walker makes him march with all his antennas of attention and awareness agog. His attitude is most different from "doing nothing". He summons a constant banquet for the eyes and for reflection… remaining calm, as though enjoying the food dishes, but from a distance, without getting to taste them materially, only through their aroma. Equipped with not so small a memory, the sight acts as the shutter of a camera—it is something like the French photographer Henri Cartier-Bresson's famous "decisive moment". It is a privileged moment of observation, after countless visual experiences of large trace, which knows when to stop the flow of everything with the hand on the camera, pressing the shutter. But in this case, there are no photos on the film, nor on paper to see them enlarged. The one who walks with this detached but attentive attitude, does it with a bottomless memory, and everything happens at the mental plane, with no other support than the images. In the blink of an eye, the crazy race of everyday life stops. It means freezing a moment that for some reason he considers precious, and if not grabbed in mental snapshot, would be lost irretrievably.

This attitude implies approaching the city as a museum. It is to consider and feel it as an open museum, in more than a wild sense, as are places such as cemeteries, such as abandoned factories, large train stations, and central markets, once they have ceased in their activity. It is then, after their productive inertia, when they most clearly show their spaces and elements as art or archaeological pieces. To carry out this art and discipline, it is important to have a good sense of direction, which, however, does not guarantee anyone not getting lost in a huge city such as New Delhi, just like someone could get lost in the forest.

Open to what I may find, I was not usually on the trail of anything specific or preset, but on whatever caught my attention. A kind of repleteness, at the same time a vacuum of history was at work—the accumulation of all that this city has passed through, so old to the North, and so new to the South. In Old Delhi everything is public and open passage. From the way people act, to how the spaces are constituted, however small they may be. Nothing is private or reserved in the midst of such bluster and sound! Neither are conversations intimate, nor is there occasion for confidences in this, what once was Shahjahanabad. In contrast in New Delhi, in the south, everything happens behind closed doors, in the bungalows. Outside one cannot see anything except the arrival or departure of the cars in the large tree lined avenues, watched by soldiers in their watchtowers, who become a part of the landscape as they observe the passing traffic, or the guards from their barricades at the gates of the huge mansions.

I perceived both spaces, Old Delhi, and the new city, as two large mirrors placed with their backs to each other. The first emerges as a great Mughal era labyrinth, very rundown, extremely polluted by the new needs of a city in a flurry, and New Delhi, of British design, exactly the opposite—anti-labyrinth, with the rational distribution of its avenues, always radial, perpendicular or parallel. It is a real garden city, where following any of its evergreen, tree-lined streets, one encounters a fluid continuity, and one can easily find one's way out. Daughters of two distinct, although successive, empires, Mughal and British, both cities are uniform in their surfaces. Under them surely exists a subterranean, sensuous, sensual world of a very different nature which escapes, and which is hidden from the foreign rambler, however sensitive he may be.

To whatever extent one is surrounded by mobiles, exhaust pipes, and other electronic elements typical of the 21st century, all my walks there took me essentially to a vanished time. I felt like a contemporary urban spectator, but present in another era, at other staggered, discontinuous times. Inward, outward… Paradoxically, the more I went into the labyrinths of the alleys, the tiny shops, the more my inner turmoil cleared and lightened. It was like getting into my own entrails and untangling a deep knot! What these long wanderings always had, was something unmistakably therapeutic, balsamic, like taking a mental antibiotic that immunized me against everything that is unfavourable

These unchoreographed matinal excursions were partly prepared for—like being well informed about the history and other facts—and partly spontaneous, "a blind walk" taking things as I came upon them, led by instinct, by sight, and skin. Quite like a bewildered observer, distracted successively by different objects or locations of the troubled waters of the old Shajahanabad, I felt like a fisherman casting his nets on shoals of gleaming and varied fish.

I did not ever deviate too much from my path, which I had vaguely traced in my mind, to end up in this or that place. The truth is that it worked in my favour since I knew how to orient myself well, which guaranteed a proper channelling of my steps, though sometimes there were unexpected detours. This although I had an acceptable geographical perception of location, as also a great concentration when walking. I always believed that the sense of orientation is innate, although with practice, one gets to improve the spatial sensibility somewhat. The first thing is to be clear where the sun rises, where the East is—from there, the other three cardinal points fall into place automatically. Guided usually by the sun, all living beings, animals and plants, have a sense of direction, which helps them locate themselves in space, and over generations and centuries, take on the habits and features that constitute them as this or that genre.

The seasoned wanderer specializes in knowing how to get lost, which does not mean that he is disoriented. During his ambulation, he enjoys the crowd, the public space, the movement, and the most varied colours. Although in private places, when he sits and gathers his thoughts on what he just saw, he requires solitude, and does not want to be interrupted. Knowing that he is always on the go, he makes very few personal ties, travelling carefree around all places, only as an observer, not as a protagonist. If he were to put an excess of emotional burden on his travels, he would hardly be able to walk! The passer-by does not like to be recognized or fall into routine relations, become a patron of anything or anyone while frequenting places with an established regularity. He would have to stop and be attentive to each person! Look at the tangle of each one's own and non-transferable circumstances, each drama or need. His interest is something so abstract and yet so concrete as the city as a whole, the strong and continuous pulse it emits!

I read extensively about the city, its two poles, its two most identifiable axes, Shahjahanabad and New Delhi. I actually perceived the two Delhis like hearts, like two sibling bodies, similar and yet opposed to each other. What I did was to drink from both of the fountains until they became communicating vessels, reversible, despite the immense distance that separates them, not in space but in time and in aesthetics. Also, somewhere between the two, on the time-line, is a fact that dominates the perception of their inhabitants and makes both cities so different.

This is located at the point in the 15th century, when the Renaissance began in the West, when the spatial representation perspective made the perception of space and the architectural context vary radically. It forced everything to be more visual, and more linear. It happened to the detriment of the other senses and movements. Till then, everything had been more intuitive in the approach to the city, closer to the level of the senses—the smells, the colours, the textures, and sounds…that often exchanged their roles giving whimsically strange mixes between them.

If there is one place in Delhi that abundantly defines the confluence of the most varied religions and cultures of India, it is the area in front of Lahore Gate of the Red Fort, the short space that runs from there to the so-called Spice Market, nestled in Chandni Chowk. In little more than five hundred metres we find on the left side a Jain temple, followed by a Hindu temple, then a Sikh Gurudwara, and finally a huge mosque though it goes unnoticed, and in front of these is the Central Baptist Church. This concentration of places of worship is so explicit, so overwhelming, representative of almost all Indian religions, excluding the very small Jewish and Parsi minorities, that nobody seems to overtly notice it. As a matter of fact the Jewish and Parsi religions never had an implantation in Delhi, being confined to coastal lands of the south, in Kerala and Bombay, Maharashtra.

Facing the ramparts of the Red Fort, and housing the famous Bird Hospital, perhaps the only one in the world, is the Lord Digambar Jain Lāl Mandir, the oldest and perhaps the best-known Jain temple in New Delhi. This sui generis dispensary, of bright colours, and built in its current form in the fifties of the last century, is a must visit for anyone who wants to know Old Delhi. It has limited resources, but it is endearing to see the treatment given here to wounded birds. It is said that the birds are picked up by practitioners of this religion, whose priests wear masks all the time so as not to risk swallowing even a single insect, and one of its sects, the Digamabaras, walk totally naked, with symbolically, no possessions. From the entrance one can see several people, middle aged men and women, around small tables, or on the ground, mending with great dedication, broken wings, splinting legs, repairing cuts and putting them into small cages. They hope that this way they will recover, or at least they will not be attacked by other animals outside, or squashed in the ruthless city traffic.

This old Jain temple was built in 1658 by the same emperor who created this city, Shah Jahan, who generously invited upon several Agrawali Jain merchants, from Haryana and Rajasthan, to settle here. He offered them land in this area, not far from where the Yamuna used to flow. Even now innumerable havelis of rich Jain merchants can still be seen between the Dariba Kalan silver market, and the Kinari Bazar paper market. Sadly almost all of them are now in ruins. However their beautiful columns and chiselled hard stone or sandstone facades with intricate vegetal motifs are carefully conserved. Hopefully one day these historic mansions will be rescued from oblivion and grime, from dust and ruin! The place will then get a completely different look! There has already been a first attempt with one haveli becoming a hotel!

Inside the Śrī Digambar temple, there are important marble and alabaster statues of the first Tirthankara Rishabhanatha, and of Parshvanath, the predecessor of Mahavira, the only historically attested teacher and creator of Jainism. Of the twenty-four recognized gurus, whose only goal was liberation from all human condition, most were purely legendary, and not historical. On the first floor, where the sacred part of the temple is located, there are elongated tables, in the manner of small shrines, with a profusion of candles and flower offerings. They are approached mostly by women, who pass their hands over the candles, lightly touching the flame with their palms. The immense respect and adoration for the elements and cosmology without god is striking, based as it is on a hermetic and extreme philosophy, difficult to understand from the perspective of monotheist beliefs.

A little further on from Sri Digambar we find a Hindu temple known as Gauri Shankar Mandir, with a newly built entrance, which conceals the oldest part, some three hundred years old, behind the stairs. Like a world axis, a dark brown Shiva-Lingam, on a female *padma*, is located centrally in the sanctum sanctorum of this temple. Everywhere, on its resplendent Makrana marble walls, we can see representations of scenes from the life of Lord Shiva, his wife Parvati, and his faithful bull Nandi. In two or three shrine showcases of silver, one can see snakes, a totemic animal associated with Shiva just like the bull. Suns converted into open and generous lotuses, into trees of life, and scenes of the great god of destruction and renewal, complete this sanctuary.

According to legend, it was a Maratha soldier of the Deccan, Apa Gangadhar, a devotee of Shiva seeing himself close to death during a battle, offered to build a shrine to his beloved Lord of the Yogis if his life was saved… Both of which, defying even the most likely destiny, did happen. This place, which has several historical gems of great value, is always full of devotees and visitors, both from the city and from distant villages. Below, at the entrance, there are several garland vendors, who also sell bananas, fruits, and rice, for the offering (puja). Monday is the day special to the god, and considered the most auspicious of the week. So different a culture from that of today's office-goers, who hate Mondays!

Continuing on the same sidewalk of Chandni Chowk, we reach the Gurdwara Sis Ganj Sahib, one of the most important historic Sikh temples in New Delhi. Its construction was initiated by Baghel Singh, the Sikh military leader who entered Delhi with his warriors in 1783, and occupied the Diwan-i-Am. The Mughal Emperor of the moment, Shah Alam II, was forced to sign a concession for practitioners of this religion to build a gurdwara in the city, at the site of the martyrdom of the ninth Guru, Tegh Bahadur. The guru had been beheaded in 1675 by the order of the fanatic Emperor Aurangzeb, for refusing to convert to Islam. It was largely from that moment that this religious community reluctantly converted into a warrior community, as a painful defense mechanism to prevent its own disappearance. This is undoubtedly the most tolerant and least fanatical religion. The Sikhs are warriors, yet they are never aggressive or exhibitionist.

There in Sis Ganj Sahib, there is a kind of basement, with a historic fountain from which Guru Tegh Bahadur drank water and washed himself before being killed along with his followers. There is also the trunk of the tree under which he was beheaded. In this constricted space, marked by narrow streets, it is understandable that this gurdwara does not have a lake, like other important gurdwaras, similar to the great Golden Temple of Amritsar. In this place of great fervour, I entered one day in the middle of the morning, and I heard an attractive and repetitive melody accompanying the prayers of the believers. I listened for a while to the three musicians, one playing the tabla, another the harmonium, and the third chanting beautiful verses. The devotional music of Sikhism, called kirtan, has points in common with the Hindustani raga and taal. Sung in praise of God by the faithful, kirtan constitutes the daily devotional songs raised to the divinity.

Emerging from Hinduism, the Sikh faith shares some concepts with this majority religion in India, such as the reincarnation of the soul in different forms until it reaches perfection. That is when the fusion of the individual atman or soul occurs with an unnamed God, synonymous with Eternal Truth and Creator of all that exists as a small light that dissolves in the Celestial Light. Sikhism does not, however, share the caste system, and it is the guru who makes the absolute Being known.

Practitioners of this religion of service, converted into the faith of peaceful warriors, grew more and more in Punjab, which occurred in parallel to the fanaticism of the last great Mughal emperor, Aurangzeb who was responsible for the death of the ninth guru Teg Bahadur. Something that would be a "before and after" in this community that wanted to individually and collectively shed fear. That is why the tenth and last guru, Gobind Singh, imposed the five "K" obligations, so that they do not forgot that they are Sikh: *kesh*—uncut hair, *kangha*—comb, hygiene and discipline, *kara*—steel bracelet, which symbolically points to the protection of the warrior, *kirpan*—dagger to defend himself, not attack, and *kachcha* or *kachera*—cotton underpants.

Entering the Fatehpuri Masjid, erected in the name of Fatehpuri Begum, one of the wives of the Mughal Emperor Shah Jahan, is isolating yourself from the noise and chaos that reigns in the area. This place, on Khari Baoli Road, formerly had pools and tanks for the supply of water to the city. Around it, there is a bazar packed with shops and stalls selling all kinds of spices, dry fruits, and the most varied pickles. This market is also known as Gadodia Market, as it was apparently erected by a merchant by that name in the 1920s. The British closed and sold the mosque after the Mutiny of 1857, and it was reopened as a mosque in 1877. Inside the Fatehpuri mosque, the silence seems an illusion. For outside is the roar of traffic and amid the thousands of spice stands, you can find old Mughal recipes for medicines for the treatment of flu, a bad stomach ache or headache.

Medicines that range from simple common and ordinary plants to mixtures of more complicated and exotic elements such as drinkable silver and other strange remedies. Along with this are found the "normal" dry fruits, nuts, figs, almonds, tamarinds and tisanes, herbal tea concoctions.

While meandering through the streets of that area of Old Delhi, I watched carefully and with great respect, the people working in the stores and small workshops, manufacturing paper, metals, or colourful objects used in weddings and festivities: Krishna crowns, multicoloured cordage, confetti, scarves, and garlands—they occupy one whole bazar. Something that should certainly win all Guinness awards for exclusivity is the number of establishments that design and print wedding invitations, not just dozens but hundreds of them. Imagination is unleashed in unsuspected ways in these cards, given the importance that weddings have here, mediated almost always by astrologers. Invitations to weddings in the rest of the planet are offered with a sober paper card in a simple envelope. Here, you will find all conceivable types of ornamentation, European Baroque, imitating the Versace style, or motifs with Hindu roots, such as Arjuna on a chariot going into battle, along with scenes from the Mahabharata or Ramayana, with figures of Krishna, Ganesha, and Hanuman among others. Sometimes, the decoration is of great taste and originality, with surprising tones and contrasts, pistachio green, indigo blue, saffron orange, and intensely gilded, while others appear unnecessarily cluttered.

Each week this repeated meandering turned for me into exercising the "art of the passer-by", with me becoming a kind of urban pioneer. In addition to the groups and casual tourist couples, betrayed by their shorts and the striking colours of their uniformed outfits, I never met in my wanderings any other expatriate resident like me, someone who took advantage of a holiday to kick the dust in the city. That's what I did almost obsessively, with no set but clear and precise rules, improving them with every new day. From one place to another, I saw such walks as a collage, effectively collating and mentally assembling very different materials, times, and places, blending as in a work of liquid art… Disseminated!

Yes, I would transform into some kind of improvised detective on the trail not of individuals but of havelis, buildings, or architectural elements, as also of buddhas and ancient bronzes, or sometimes not even that. The big and the small, the concrete and the diffuse, everything that had to do with this place, Delhi, found favour in my steps, an endearing space. Despite non-stop reading and informing myself, I did not make advance plans for my outings, nor did I carry a camera, a map, or protect myself with a hat, sunglasses, and the usual bottle of mineral water. None of those tourist defences and shelters for me! I rejected them explicitly!

Many days, sitting on the veranda of my house at sunset, I used to enjoy a privileged view of the crows—how they covered with their flight the entire sky of the Zoo, which stretched out in front of the garden. Dozens, sometimes even hundreds of them, formed a blanket that would cover the sky completely. Some floated as if they were kites, hovering around, and then swooping from a great height towards the trees. Others plowed the air in the four cardinal directions, in linear grooves.

In the morning too, the squawking crows would wake me up me at the first light of dawn. But they no longer sounded aggressive, nor did they seem to bring bad omens, as they had appeared to do when I was living in the farm house. Yes, it was a great pleasure that I was no longer agitated by the cawing of the crows, or the various sounds of birds in general, that had earlier seemed threatening.

Contrary to the bad reputation it had been given, the crow is an intelligent and smart bird. His flight is straight, always balanced and elegant. He often draws wide curves in the air, always labouring firmly, with wings and tail well extended in order to achieve a solid support. He stops to observe, and when he knows he is being observed, he likes it very much. He does not flee, because he loves the mutual recognition with his peers, but also with humans and other animals, because his curiosity is boundless. The eyes are in command! He halts a few moments near the stroller, letting him know of his presence with his eyes before escaping. He takes a few short steps, measuring the direction well, and then continues with hesitant jumps, to once again fly off… Towards the highest point!

Not in vain, he is one of the most named birds in the Bible, and for the ancient Greeks he was essentially the prophetic bird, consecrated to Apollo as a vehicle of knowledge of the night, much as the swan was of the day. The Roman augurs distinguished more than seventy different crow squawks. For them, interpreting the language of crows meant being able to penetrate the occult, to predict what was to happen, as was their task, sending out omens after listening to them in order to either initiate or avoid an action, be it referring to daily life, or to decisive issues of State such as undertaking a battle.

The eternal opposition of the biblical and Judeo-Christian world between the white dove, symbol of peace, innocence and purity, against the black crow, who with his colour had all the black connotations, is well known. The ancient Greeks and Romans, though, identified the crow with the sun. Indeed, both in Greece and Rome, the bird was associated with Athena and Apollo, symbols of sunlight and wisdom. It is true that he also had the role of Charon, who in Greek mythology goes with his boat ferrying the souls to the other side of life, a belief shared by India. Crows in Indian culture are deemed to possess valuable information, they are provided with a great memory and also have the role of transporting souls, linked to the world of the ancestors, of whom they are messengers.

In Sanskrit, the crow has innumerable names such as *karati, kaaga, kaaka, vaayasa, balibhoja, balipusta, malabhuj,* and *vanaváasin*. Since it appears as the bird that communicates with the hidden world and the mysterious, that is, with the other side of life, with death, it is considered the vehicle of Shani, elder brother of Yama, god of Death. Shani Dev considered by many as an avatar, a personification of Shiva, symbolizes misfortune and melancholy linked to human life, and is perhaps one of the most misunderstood deities of Hindu mythology, with very few temples dedicated to him, except for those in northern Rajasthan. In Vedic astrology, the planet Saturn is known as Shani, which in Sanskrit literally means "moving slowly".

For a really long time, almost since adolescence, I have been an ardent lover of Indian cuisine. As proof of that, whenever I travel to a city, the first thing I find out is whether there are good restaurants with a menu in the region's specialty, and often they are the first ones I visit. While in Spain, prior to my departure for New Delhi my mouth used to water thinking of the Indian dishes I would be able to eat almost every day...naan and chutney and pickles of the most diverse types—mango, ginger, garlic, lime, and others. I imagined, when I came here, that I was going to have all possible curries, with which to satisfy my desire for new taste experiences in this immense food paradise. And indeed, I did it conscientiously, especially during the first months, with all the imaginable varieties of lamb curries, of the rogan josh type, whether with yogurt, spinach, with or without nuts, light or thick consistency, semi-sweet or salty. Almost every day I went at noon to my favourite restaurants, the classic ones of Connaught Place, such as the Embassy, or the Central Coffee House, or other more recent ones in the area, such as Veda and Azzafran.

As it happens with many words, for example, saying tuk tuk for rickshaw, instantly denotes that he or she is a foreigner! Similarly with the word "curry". Nobody here actually uses the term curry! No Indian says, 'I'm going to make a curry!" Interestingly, in the West it is believed that curry is a spice, or a kind of mixture of spices—something "already there", pre-prepared, when in reality it involves a process of grinding the "masala"...a mixture of anything between five to twenty different spices, starting with the best known ones, such as cinnamon, clove, cardamom, cumin, coriander seed, mustard, turmeric, red chilli, peppercorn, and occasionally nutmeg and anise.

It is commonly believed that the curries here are usually quite hot. This is often largely true. But not all curries need be spicy! I usually tried to communicate to the waiters and chefs, the two concepts of "spicy", one that is replete with a range of spices in the perfect proportion imparting an intense aroma and a deep flavour, and "hot" with an excess of the chilli or cayenne or whatever, factor. This spice which binds you to Mexico...best to leave it there! It is something that I tried to explain in all possible ways. But in vain. Was it that hard to understand? It simply comes down to not putting chilli, cayenne, or whatever you want to call it, in the masala!

One can only imagine what Babur and the first Mughal chieftains must have felt on crossing the Indus and entering the rich Kashmir valley after traversing the famous Khyber Pass. His love for Srinagar and its surroundings with its unfamiliar fauna and flora is eminently evident. He and his tribesmen must have thought they had reached paradise itself! What they wanted was not only to recreate, but to surpass the much admired Iranian cities such as Isfahan. These lands were greener owing to the fresh water from the thaw of the Himalayan snows, but their poets had employed the same metaphors and descriptions in the real and imaginary gardens conceived by them. It was then a magical land, something that is reflected in the books of Italian and Arab travellers of the time, such as Ludovico di Vaterna and Al Biruni. Hindustan, in short, became for these cultured conquerors their own land, a wonderful find appropriated and recreated in its topography, its trees and mountains, its birds, its music. The Baburnamah, a great biographical book done in the Persian manner of the Book of Kings, illustrates the great fascination Babur had for the land he had found.

These Turkic tribes were strongly Iranian, so for several centuries Iran, in its culture and its forms, along with its language, would remain the ideal in this conquered land. However, upon entering India, the Mughal leaders, their families and companions, were dazzled and captivated by this vast region stretching from the Himalayas, the Gangetic plain, and the two converging coasts on both sides of the Deccan plateau. They were well aware that they were facing an exuberant, complex, and ancient civilization, with great treasures, material and intangible, something that surpassed theirs. It is quite amazing that a small Central Asian family could create an empire that achieved unparalleled splendour, lasting for a century and a half.

In a very short space of time after the arrival of the Mughals in the Indian subcontinent, Persian, the new language, began to be spoken in places as far from its origins as Agra, Lahore, Delhi, and Lucknow. The Persian script nastaliq would be adopted, with its aerial paragraphs, that seem to float beautifully in the lines of the texts, alongside the celebrated colourful miniatures. In a more popular register than the cosmopolitan and diplomatic Persian language, Urdu, the language of the army was generated, with a neo-Sanskrit grammar but Iranian and Arabic vocabulary. Parallel to these changes brought about by the foreign power, was the increasing influence of myriad artists, warriors, dignitaries, poets who continuously came to the Indian cities from Merv or Isfahan.

Humayun (1530–1556) was not to become an accomplished military strategist like his father, Babur, since from the beginning he was attracted to poetry and contemplative pleasures of the palace, such as opium. However, it was he who actually established the pillars of the Mughal Empire, founding the new capital in Delhi, while conferring on his lineage a fine mix of diverse Iranian arts, but with a marked Indian identity. All this was a consequence of being defeated (1540) by the Afghan warrior Sher Shah. Humayun went into exile in Iran for fifteen years, then recovered Delhi in 1555. By a strange quirk of fate, only six months later he would die in the most absurd manner, tripping on the stairs of his library. During his long Iranian exile, however, he did not waste time, because when he returned to India he brought with him various musicians, calligraphers, and painters, who largely decided the future of what we now know as Mughal art, and by extension Indian art, in one of its highest expressions. Khawaja Abdul Samad and Mir Sayyid Ali, were, for example, the painters who would introduce the illuminated miniatures of the Safavid style beyond the Indus, the same ones that even today astonish all those who contemplate them for their beauty and refinement, even though their conservation in museums and palaces, in many cases leaves much to be desired. Anyone who observes them, can in fact check the resemblance with their Safavid predecessors of Iran, for whom it was not a taboo to be figurative, something prevalent in much of the Muslim world, due to a distorted interpretation of the *ayat*s of the Quran that defines Allah as the One who "gives form" to living beings. In the Mughal case, as well as in its Iranian precedent, the features are not only realistic, but suggest the artists and painters enjoyed the forms of nature, both plant and animal, and especially people. Only the holy ones, the Prophet and his family, appear faceless, usually their heads surrounded with flames, out of respect for their divinized features.

It would have to be his son, Akbar, who would be known by posterity as the Great Mughal, extremely long-lived in his reign lasting half a century, a tireless builder, as well as an energetic promoter of the arts, music, miniature painting, and like his grandfather Babur, a great lover of gardens. Born in 1543 in the Sind, now in Pakistan, Akbar was crowned emperor at 13 years of age. What lay ahead for him was the extension of the Empire to the South and the East coast, weaving truly strategic alliances, many of them matrimonial, with the Hindu Rajput princes, whom he appointed generals of his own armies, thus holding their possible aspirations in check, while taking advantage of their local control. Instead of fighting against the Rajput princes of Bengal, Sind, and Orissa, among other places, Akbar appointed them as his generals, and made them feel they were part of the great Mughal Empire, they being the most successful ones. Something very similar to what subsequently the British would do with the Maharajas across India, thus ensuring the loyalty of many small kingdoms of Rajasthan and other places.

Akbar from the beginning showed a desire to integrate all religious communities of India, including the minorities, such as Christians and Parsis, but mainly did so with the Hindus and Muslims, something that transcended into the architecture and the other arts of his times. Among the progressive measures, the Great Mughal abolished the tax that non-Muslims paid for not professing this religion, which was in force since the establishment of the Sultanate a long time ago. The first cadastre, a public register with details of ownership of the real property of a given area, used for tax assessment was set up by him. He also created a rational system of taxes for agricultural land. Despite his many conquests, with which he brought much of the Deccan Plateau under his dominion, it was this cancellation of tax on Hindus and other religions that largely won him the sympathy of the local population, because it was seen as an act of respect for other religions. This, and other similar wise decisions, form much of the basis of contemporary India, a difficult balance between very different identities…something that the current rulers, ultranationalists, should not forget in their policies and attitudes.

The golden and stable period in the half century long reign of Akbar is undoubtedly the fourteen years he lived in Fatehpur Sikri. When the emperor inexplicably left its red ramparts, where according to all the chronicles, he had been very happy, the place became deserted forever, like a ghost town, according to the European travellers and missionaries of the moment. It would take a long time before Lord Curzon (Viceroy of India between 1899 and 1905) and the British restored it as a palace-museum. Without being only Muslim or only Hindu, this is the first palatial city totally Indian in its style. It is a kind of non-denominational architectural style which would serve as a model for subsequent constructions of the Mughal Empire. There were certain motifs in that new canon, some Indian, such as the lotus, the sculpted pillars, the *chhatri*, or small canopy-like structures on the rooftops, the domes of Buddhist inspiration, as well as the inscriptions and geometric ornaments from Iran and the Arab world. Fatehpur Sikri is a magnificent conjunction of massive red sandstone and a non-negligible presence of white marble, which gives it a very elegant counterpoint of textures and colours. It always awaits us there as a utopian city, of a strange modernity, endowed with diverse Iranian and Buddhist influences, in addition to the Hindu and Muslim roots.

Besides the obligatory military campaigns, Akbar greatly enjoyed hunting, nature, sports, acquiring rare and unique objets d"art, something that brought him closer to European Renaissance princes, at the same time that Philip II reigned in Spain. Like his peers many miles away, Akbar was also a great administrative reformer. He divided his administration into four clearly differentiated "ministries"—military, economic, religious affairs, and internal affairs. He brought about economic reforms, remarkably improving the infrastructure as was seen in the intense construction of roads and ports not seen since the times of Emperor Ashoka nineteen centuries earlier… Almost two thousand years ago! His son Jahangir, hedonistic and indolent, was a far cry from his illustrious father. In these vast lands there had been no emperor like Akbar. Nobody had done anything similarly significant in the communications network of this vast and varied subcontinent.

Fatehpur Sikri was erected in an area called Saik, meaning a place with water, known even in the early days of the Mahabharata (1,200 BC), which is ironical as today it is practically dry most of the year. We are used to guides and books repeating that Fatehpur Sikri was abandoned without apparent explanation, probably because they ran out of water. Although many chronicles of the time attest that there were several reservoirs there, and a lake, which apparently was full at that time. Besides it seems unlikely that such a huge architectural project would have been undertaken for three decades, without an assessment of the minimum amount of water supply available. More likely the abandonment was because the throne was going through an internal war at that time motivated by the pretensions of Akbar's stepbrother Mirza Muhammad Hakim. Also, his son Jahangir was contesting the throne. This combination of circumstances had probably forced Akbar to seek a good defensive shelter, something that the palace did not possess, built only for rest and pleasure, and the cultivation of the arts.

One of the reasons for having erected such a fabulous city there was that the emperor, unable to produce a male heir, put himself in the hands of a reputed Sufi saint, residing in that place. His name was Salim Chishti, through whose intercession and prayers, according to legend, his first son was finally born, the future Jahangir. The latter was also given the name Salim, after the saint who had prophesied his birth. This was why he built a great mosque and in its immense courtyard he placed the glittering tomb of the saint, such was his gratitude for having saved the Mughal dynasty. The charged atmosphere one breathes in the interior is soul-stirring, amidst the tombs of the descendants, on which light filters through the white marble lattices in enigmatic patterns.

The repeated conflicts that are noticed in the matter of succession in the Mughal dynasty come from the Timurid custom of seizing power by force, fighting with one's brothers or cousins, disregarding the right of the eldest son of the dead or deposed king, the theoretical continuator of the lineage. The truth is that in general, Muslim dynasties always had such problems because they were polygamous. This invariably led to automatic confrontation at the time of succession between different branches of the family, with the same father, irrespective of there being a named successor. The throne was never assured!

A few kilometres away from Fatehpur Sikri, the Red Fort of Agra, on the banks of the river Yamuna, did offer Akbar a solid shelter for himself and his army, equipped as it was with 22 meter high walls. However the interior was dominated by pleasant pavilions and gardens. This fort would be the model for several such fortifications as in Lahore and Allahabad and later become the inspiration for his grandson Shah Jahan in Delhi. Such was its splendour! Indeed, though he had devoted himself to raising Fatehpur Sikri, Akbar was throughout his reign an "emperor builder", and had not abandoned the construction of the forts of Agra and Lahore. The truth is that Sikander Lodi, the most well-known exponent of the ruling dynasty previous to the Mughals, had already begun to build the future capital of the empire in Agra, but when his son Ibrahim was defeated by Babur (in 1526), in the well-known and decisive Battle of Panipat, the latter continued with the ambitious project, making it his capital, so as to be, in fact, closer to his Rajput enemies, spread throughout Central India and the Deccan.

After the sudden exit of Akbar to Agra only a military cantonment remained, and that too was finally dismantled when Shah Jahan transferred the capital of the empire to the present day Delhi, giving it the name of Shahjahanabad. The palaces so enjoyed in another time, and the luminous dargah of very white marble would be cared for by the descendants of saint Salim Chisti, who had unwittingly been responsible for all that construction. Few cities and palaces in the world are as identified with their creator as Fatehpur Sikri is with Akbar, erected to his measure and endowed with a very elaborate ceremonial court that included ambassadors from distant countries, musicians, poets, artists, mercenaries, and a long list of inhabitants, visitors, and residents. A detailed account of all this is given by the Spanish Jesuit Antonio Monserrate who along with the Italian Rodolfo Acquaviva spent some years in the prodigious red city, thinking that they could convert Akbar to Christianity.

If you go to this amazing place between October and April, ahead of the heat that makes it a dry land, it is a pleasure to wander through its silent and amazing courtyards, built in elegant straight lines that transfigure their marbles and red sandstones. You can easily imagine the wasteland the place must have been, before becoming the famous palatial city in all its splendour. The architects, engineers, artisans and workers who had recently erected the Agra Fort, almost all of them Hindus, came mostly from the newly conquered Gujarat. Even before the construction of the city was completed, Akbar and his family were living there along with his courtiers and army. Fatehpur Sikri was to Akbar the dreamed Samarkand of his (Timur) ancestors, the same one that so many times had been reconstructed in the mind by his grandfather Babur, with gardens, fountains, and palaces, surrounded by musicians, miniaturists, and courtiers from many different places.

The continued attempt to transcend the numerous difficulties of becoming the ruler of a land with innumerable religions and races, castes and sacred places, contained in an immeasurable geography, consolidated in the person of Akbar, a man with a great vision. Seen from a current perspective, Akbar appears on many planes as someone really advanced for his time. Perhaps he is the first Indian ruler who really wanted to belong to all his subjects without distinction, from the mountainous North to the deep South, passing through the ghats of both coasts. In that sense, he was also the initiator of his own native architecture, Mughal-Rajput, with many different roots originating from Samarkand to Istanbul, from the Deccan to Afghanistan. He created roads and infrastructure that were intended to last for centuries to come, and that indeed exist even today throughout the entire Indian geography. From Delhi to Agra, from Kabul to Srinagar, through Lahore, in addition to the many other cities named, he literally went about creating the fabric of the empire as he advanced his military campaigns towards the centre of the subcontinent, as also towards the unexplored East and South. He assumed his role to perfection, as dynamic as it was syncretic, in all fields, to create a new inclusive Indian society, in which Islam played an important civilizing role, although it was not the only one. The eclectic, but well defined architecture, the music, bright and full in all its genres, the open religion, the splendid Iranian-based literature, in addition to the very rich applied arts, were his "soft power" as a key for legitimisation, sought not only through weapons and conquests in such a vast and varied land.

The "Great Mughal", as Akbar would be known through centuries, did not stop for more than a few weeks, or at most a couple of months in the same place. In fact, he was also motivated by seasonal changes throughout the year. In summer, he tended to remain in Srinagar, while the rest of the time, between March and October, was spent around Agra. His palaces were built with that tireless rhythm! It must have been impressive to see him move when he was leaving for some distant place, because apart from the army, he regularly travelled with a 100 elephants, 500 camels and many other escort soldiers, in addition to a total of 2,000 people to erect the camps and attend to him. He was indeed the Great Mughal par excellence!

Despite being a warrior, Akbar must have been a man of exquisite taste and a deep understanding of any reality or situation. He was aware that there is something that masks the ultimate reality of the universe, which is one, and which we do not know. And it was in that he invested a good part of his efforts. Among other ingenuities of an exploratory and advanced mind in various fields, and to implement his thoughtful plan of interreligious conversations, in 1575, Akbar built a place known as *Ibādat Khāna* (House of Worship) in Fatehpur Sikri. Inspired perhaps by Sufi Mirza Sulaiman Kirani of Bengal, a pioneer in spiritual debates, The House of Worship basically consisted of a room where, periodically, and under the watchful eye of the emperor, leaders of different religious groups, Hindus, Christians, Muslims, Parsis, Jains, atheists (as can be seen in the lively and colourful miniatures of the time) met to discuss both their varied beliefs and doctrinal peculiarities, as well as their common points. All beliefs, with an important community of practitioners in the Indian subcontinent, had a place there. For, in religion no one holds the unique Truth! Among the several Jesuits who also participated, was the Spanish priest Antonio de Monserrate. He spent a long time in Fatehpur Sikri, and many courtly details of this magnificent city-palace appear in his memoirs.

As is known, as learned throughout history, we all tend to build our gods in our image and likeness. Evidence of this great tolerance with other religions is that Jodha Bai, the mother of Akbar's successor, Jahangir, was apparently a Jodhpur princess, and therefore Hindu. The beginning of such conversations and contributions to this project of understanding, must have been really exciting, since these meeting spaces, both physical and mental, were not at all evident in the daily activity of their Islamic and Hindu societies, but shone as pearls, as diamonds, when they were found. What an atmosphere must there have been in such a place! Of lights and abstracted shadows!

The most notable features that emerged in Hinduism were Vedic ritualization and the search for liberation from the chain of reincarnations. In Islam, on the other hand, the absolute Unity of God prevailed, and the "surrender" of the believer, to Him. In Christianity, some of the key links were mercy, salvation, and resurrection. Just as in Buddhism, it was the deepening of meditation as a way to free oneself from desire and obtain the "extinction" of the self, emptied, in the emptiness of Being.

Throughout these intense encounters and conversations, Akbar begins to devise a kind of religion, or rather, a new angle from which to contemplate and experience such long-standing religions. It was a fusion of apparent opposites, Islam and Hinduism, which started from very different habits and beliefs. The *Dīn-i Ilāhī*, "the Religion of God", as Akbar baptized the new syncretic faith, was destined to become the referent of a new society, as hybrid in the religious as in the social aspect. It was not really an unknown religion, or an absolute novelty, but it was a summary and clarification of certain confluences of the mysticism of Islam-Sufism, with Hinduism. *Dīn-i Ilāhī* was a brave and firm experiment of reconciliation and coming together! Maybe the first time something like this had happened in the world!

Despite his good intentions and despite having the instruments of power, Akbar failed in his attempt to devise a new form of shared religion. Perhaps he limited himself to comparing elements considered different to begin with…like parallel rivers, close but separate, that finally did not converge in a common course. Perhaps if he had started from the common truths, in the beating heart of both religions, and how it manifests itself in their rituals and beliefs, he might have reached something lasting, as it happened in more contemporary times with Sikhism, that even today has great vigour and spiritual energy. Although his basic idea did not succeed, it contained great power—the assertion that much more united them than made them different. Time and the reality of confrontation between the two deactivated that possible project of understanding, but it was exactly at the point where Akbar failed, that his great-grandson Dara Shikoh started a herculean attempt to overcome the strict monotheism of Islam, and the elastic polytheism of Hinduism. Dara Shikoh formed the hard core of this dialogue between the mystical expressions of both religions—Vedantic monotheism, and Sufism. An interesting point of unresolved diatribe is whether Akbar was a true Muslim believer at the end of his life, or inwardly advanced in another direction.

Due to these adverse circumstances of expansion, Akbar's religion was adopted only by a score of followers, the closest friends and family. *Dīn-i Ilāhī* was the product of the fusion of apparent opposites, and therefore it was an excessively abstract improvement to be practiced. One of the reasons why it did not take root with the people, was that there were no concrete writings of such an "invented" religion, nor any monks or *mollah*s who would propagate it, since it had been conceived beyond rites and external rituals. From this frustrated desire to integrate the different communities that made up India, it seems that the famous fable of the elephant and the Mughal emperor may be apt. In this Eastern legend, a king lets enter a certain number of people in a dark room, in which an elephant has previously been introduced. In his ignorance of the objective of the experiment, one touches the trunk and believes that it is the branch of a tree… Another touches a ear and assumes that it is a fan. The third grabs the tail, and thinks it is a thick rope. One of them runs into one leg and thinks it is a column… The moral is that no one possesses totality of knowledge, only fragments of it. When light is lacking one is privy to only pasts of knowledge. For it is light that makes clear the true situation. This is indeed a metaphor for the light of knowledge, which transcends the separation of the parts, represented by darkness.

Akbar began this pioneering and painstaking activity in the energetic attempt to bring closer the two most important religious communities in India. He had in his favour the fact of being a true statesman, undoubtedly the first one in Modern India. His broad mind could accommodate the entire State as well as its institutions and challenges, its potentialities and its problems, in addition to the fabulous cluster of regions and idiosyncrasies already integrated into the Mughal Empire, and those that would eventually be. In an attempt to anticipate events, perhaps the emperor had the wise forewarning that in a distant future, almost four centuries later, there would be a great misfortune such as the partition of India in 1947, into three important fragments.

This initiative carried out by Akbar against wind and tide, defined today as interreligious dialogue, was really ahead of its time, entering fully into the field of comparative religions, something that in the western orbits would not start until much later, well into the 19th century, in fact. In the field of Akbar's European counterparts, such as Philip II, no enlightened monarch of the time was attracted to the dialogue of cultures and religions, even though they didn't lack for reasons, given the flagrant problems that arose between Catholicism and Protestantism. Rather, they were more attracted to parties, dances and oddities of the Wunderkammer, the Cabinet of curiosities.

Dara Shikoh (Dario the Great in Persian), eldest son of Mughal emperor Shah Jahan, was born in 1615 in Rajasthan, near the great Sufi shrine of Ajmer. According to legend, his father visited the tomb of the renowned Muslim saint Hazrat Moinuddin Chishti, asking for a male heir to be born to him. Exactly the same thing had happened with his great grandfather Akbar. His heir, Jahangir, was the consequence of prayers to the Sufi master Salim Chishti of Fathepur Sikri, which is why the Great Mughal built such a magnificent red city there.

Being the first born, Dara Shikoh was the presumed heir to the emperor Shah Jahan, and his favourite wife, Mumtaz Mahal, for whom the latter would build the highly acclaimed Taj Mahal. It was meant to be a tribute of love that would be remembered for centuries, and recognized throughout the world as an archetype of beauty and harmony. Even as a child, Dara showed a sensitive and contemplative character. He was educated and nurtured from a young age by Mullah Abdul Latif Saharanpuri, from whom he learned the profound basis of Islam. Later he also frequented some Hindu pandits of Benares, like Jagan Nath Misra, who counselled him and facilitated through their teachings his search for a common point between Islamic mysticism and Indian philosophy. That seemed to be his destiny, a great destiny, though soon truncated—the discovery of a middle path between two such counterpoised views of perceiving Divinity that the two faiths proffer: the rigorously Singular one and the absolutely Plural one. Indeed! He had elements in his favour that would not ever repeat themselves! History could have reserved a special role for him, of "reconciliation" between the two great and major religions of India since medieval times—Islam and Hinduism… But that was not to be!

It was absolutely unusual for a future Muslim leader to be so keenly interested in Hindu thought. Not only to soften the harshness between the leaders of the two communities, but to try and find a solid foundation of understanding and dialogue. Dara Shikoh did it with courage and determination, getting many Hindu texts translated from Sanskrit to Persian, including the Bhagavad Gita, along with excerpts from fifty Upanishads, in a book which he called *Sirr-e-Akbar* (the Great Secret). As all the children of the Mughal emperors, Dara had been educated in the Quran, and in Persian poetry, as much as in music and the applied arts, history, among others. Since his childhood he had been exposed to the influence of Sufism through Hazrat Miyan Mir (m.1635), a teacher of the Qadiri order from Lahore, whose disciple he became, and who said there was no difference between Hinduism and Islam in the "effort" to know God. Thus he would be spiritually attached to this open and liberal order, founded by Sheikh Abdul Qadir Yilani of Baghdad, and which he describes in his book *Risala-e-Haq Numa* as "the best of the ways to reach Divinity". Indian Sufism in fact shares some characteristics inspired by this mystical brotherhood, which though being monotheistic sometimes verges on pantheism, as it perceives divine presence in all things. The reason, no doubt, is that through the centuries Qadirism has been permeated by yoga, Vedanta, many ways of perception distinctive of Hindu culture. One of the common points in particular that he thought he had "discovered" was the Unity of Existence—wherever you turn you find His Face!

Majma-ul-Bahrain, the "fusion", or "Encounter of the Two Seas", Dara Shikoh's most representative book, was the result of nine years of research and intensive study along various cities in India such as Ajmer, Agra, Allahabad, Benaras, delving into the mysticism that has emerged over time in both Indian religions, Sufism and Vedanta. In this early work, he undertakes the investigation of the inner core of religions, and specifically the exploration of the common points between Hinduism and Islam. In this sense, Dara seemed to reach the conclusion that "the hidden book", which the Quran speaks of (LVI, 77–80), the one which "only the pure touch", is actually referring to the Upanishads.

As demonstrated in his text *Risala-e-Haq Numa,* he was deeply interested in Hinduism, so he moved to Benares, the great sacred city of this religion, where he studied Sanskrit, and delved especially into the Upanishads, considering them the final revelation of the Vedas. He gave form to all this in the book he wrote in Persian with the translations of the Upanishads and which he called *Sirri-i-Akbar* (The Great Secret), which was none other than the Divine unity (Al Tawhid), that he thought he had found, as shared in the Quran and the Upanishads. Another book by Dara on Sufism is *Hasanat ul-' Arifeen* (The Best of the Gnostics), composed with the sayings of a hundred Sufis from various brotherhoods, through which he delves deeply into Islamic mysticism, in order to go to the essence of its teaching. In this parallel way, he attacks the imams and clergy who, as is currently the case with violent Islam, see Islam only as a combative religion, based on a list of external rites, laws, and obligations, but without a humane quality or spiritual content.

Dara, who always had a great thirst for knowledge, was completely opposed to the orthodox and rigorist view of Islam. In fact, he had a better relationship with Hindu scholars and priests than with Muslim mullahs, despite their being representatives of his own religion. He accused them of "making a lot of noise", and not dedicating any effort to the content and spirit of their faith. He was well aware that the entire Quran is an ambiguous text, with an allegorical content, and therefore one needs to know how to interpret it, and read it as per the times, as it was compiled and written two generations after the death of the Prophet, who is perceived in the Holy Book alternatively as a mystic, and as a warrior.

When Dara Shikoh's father, Emperor Shah Jahan fell ill in 1657, succession was an open question, since although he was the rightful heir, his brother Aurangzeb, a fanatic Sunni, aimed unashamedly at the throne, finally imprisoning his father the following year in Agra Fort, where he died eight years later. Dara Shikoh fled to Punjab attempting to escape to Iran, in order to find shelter in King Shah Abbas II's court, but he was betrayed, and delivered with his son Sipar Shikoh, and two daughters, to General Bahadur Khan, who in turn sent them to New Delhi to a predictable sad end… Death. The Muslim mullahs evidently supported the usurper and managed to have Dara, accused of betrayal and infidelity, and therefore tortured and executed on direct orders from his brother Aurangzeb, in 1659.

Today the tomb of Dara Shikoh and his two children is an anonymous unmarked grave somewhere in the Humayun Tomb complex, in New Delhi. After the attempt by Dara Shikoh to unify, or at least bring closer the two major religions, there has unfortunately not been another such in India. In fact both communities moved farther and farther away, until the painful Partition of 1947, with the unexpected emergence of Pakistan, and the conflict of Kashmir deeply embedded in the life of the two countries.

Mysticism, a word that has degenerated enormously from its original meaning, is but the most immediate approach we have to the experience of the occult, of what we call sacred, because from behind a veil, mysticism transcends daily life, offering no contrast nor comparison with everyday affairs. Mysticism is about that "difficult to express experience", which provides breeze, air, and echoes from the other side of the mountain not usually treaded upon. You cannot climb such cliffs directly with your body, or at least not all the way, so as to be able to look from above at the entire landscape…such richness always escapes the eye.

Dara Shikoh was undoubtedly one of the few personalities in position of power, who recognized the historical role that religious beliefs play in the evolution of a community. He could discern the communicating vessels that exist in the underlying message, great religions have propagated over the centuries, specifically Hinduism and Islam. These are a set of beliefs, myths, legends, customs, and rites of a specific community, at a given time, for it to initiate the ascent of the spirit. Like his great-grandfather Akbar, he sensed that there are certain basic concepts which unite Hinduism and Islam in a hermetic and recondite way, even if only in their esoteric currents. That is, from the deepest and most enlightened heart of both traditions: Vedanta and Upanishad on one side, and Sufism on the other. Seen in this way, they display bridges that can be traversed!

Indeed, like his great ancestor, Akbar, Dara Shikoh, established direct contact with the Hindu sadhus, as well as with the Sufi masters, the Parsis, Christians, Buddhists, and Jains. He knew that each and every one of these creeds is embodied by a "tirtha", as the latter say, a "passage", a shortcut to be travelled and imitated, to the other side of experience. And none possesses the ultimate truth! The world of Hinduism is an endless sea that comes from the Vedas, and from the oldest mythological, philosophical, and ritual traditions created in India in parallel with them. On the one hand there is the external and visible sphere of priests and rites, and on the other, the inner face, expressed above all in the Upanishads, poetic texts of speculative philosophy about life, nature, ethics, the human body, and others. The gods of nature, of the essential elements such as Wind, Fire, Earth, Water, and Space gradually diversify, into the trinity (Brahma, Vishnu, and Shiva), next to the huge number of gods that get added to them. Hindu mysticism goes wandering, to generate thousands of deities.

On the other hand, Islam seems to always seek strict Unity, "without division". And when they minimally deviate from that path, a wave of fundamentalism happens. This is a non-negotiable principle! Something that does not exist in Hinduism, where all possible beliefs exist, from pure monotheistic to radical atheism, through all imaginable visions of deity, carnal and subtle.

The link Dara Shikoh thought he found between the message of both religious traditions, however distant they may seem to be… one, of a seemingly exuberant polytheism, and the other of a rigorous uniqueness, revealed something to him that none of the practitioners of both had ever perceived: a deep and unsuspected common plot. Such a shared path was the thirst for Unity, in one case, that of Islam, immediate and explicit Unity, and that of Hinduism, a delayed Unity, in the ultimate and all encompassing Face of an endless series of deities.

Among other characteristic elements of Sufism is the process of destruction of the ego, of personalism—"*nafs*" which is called "*faná*" that is, the extinction of the self, with the dissolution of its burden.

This is the closest thing to the Buddhist "nirvana", which literally means extinguishing the flame of a candle. After this disappearance of the particular, of the personal, for Islam what remains there is something intangible, "*baqá*", which is the divine "permanence", creation in a continuous "respite of the Merciful". It is the same, which due to its splendour entails the extinction of individuality, as the definitive return of the soul to the cosmos in Hinduism.

The Sufis maintain that God created the visible and invisible world. As a famous hadith states: "I was a hidden treasure, until I wanted to be known, and I created Creation." Likewise, the Sufis maintain that this "Continuous Creation" never concludes, since it is maintained by the divine breath, "*nafs al rahmán*", with which God Himself recreates himself in his Maximum Creation: Man! According to a famous hadith, Allah would have said: "The heavens and the earth do not embrace me, but the heart of man contains me." God created earth and the human being to reach his superior state as humanity and gave him the divine image of his names, a mirror with 99 different facets in which to look at himself.

It is through the heart, that divinity is made present. This is the place of its appearance in the human being, the crossing point between the body and the spirit. It is the mirror where the mystery is reflected, and therefore has to be cleansed by good deeds…until it shines with the light, radiated only by divinity. The obligation to burn it is the constant search of God.

Within the world of Sufi spirituality in India, the great reference is Nizamuddin Auliya (1238–1325). Like his Chishti brothers, his emphasis, in his teaching and daily work, was on love and on the life of the spirit as a means of achieving closeness to God, rather than on rituals and external gestures. He arrived in Delhi as a child, after the death of his father, with his mother, Bibi Zulekha, erecting his Dargah when he was still a youth in a quiet place on the outskirts of the Delhi Sultanate. This place, where his grave is located, is today turned into a famous and overpopulated suburb which people from all social and geographical origins frequent—merchants, to begging dervishes, local people, and those who come on their own pilgrimage from distant lands.

One of the characteristics of this Muslim mystical path, the Chishtiya, in addition to its willingness to move away from power, is that it is one of the most open ones, where it is possible to approach God in this life, without neglecting everyday existence, helping the needy, feeling compassion for the oppressed, for the sick, and the destitute. Another of its peculiarities is its proximity to the musical *samá* and the recitation of the names of God, as a way of active communion with divinity. In the same space where Nizamuddin and other relevant characters identified with his Dargah are buried, there is also the grave of the great poet Mirza Ghalib, and of Abu'l Hasan Yamīn ud-Dīn Khusrau (1253–1325). This contemporary of Dante (1265–1321) on the other side of the world, and better known as Amir Khusrau, represents the ultimate paradigm of the cultural fusion of Central Asia, imported into the Indian subcontinent. He declared himself proud to be a son of a vast Turkish-Iranian syncretic culture, proud of being a "*Turk-e-Hindustani*". It was he, in fact, with such background made up of different origins, who largely opened the way for Akbar, and his great-grandson Dara Shikoh, in that cultured and universalist vision of Islam, which even though had the support of the maximum power of the Mughal Empire, lasted unfortunately for a short period of time, to then get truncated and disappear.

Amir Khusrau, son of a Turkish Uzbek, married to the daughter of an Indian nobleman from Uttar Pradesh, is a beautiful cultural axis that unites the best of all the territories of the Middle East, from Turkey to India, through Iran and the other intermediate regions. Talented with languages, in addition to Iranian and Urdu, he spoke

Sanskrit, and by his religion, the language of the Quran, Arabic. He and Nizamuddin, the great Sufi saint, who was always his reference as a teacher, represent that open and cultured Islam that is lacking today in this and other lands. A great lover of India, especially of Delhi, he lived in a decisive, and at the same time complicated epoch, that of the Sultanate. This was a moment of great turbulence, as well as enormous cultural achievements that we still enjoy.

In his first masnawi, *Qiranu´s-Sa´dain*, he sings the wonders of the Delhi of his time, which is "like paradise on earth". He states that this capital is composed of two old cities and a new one (the fort of Kilokhari), noting the idea, in this recurring context, that there is always a latest Delhi in a long series of cities sometimes forgotten and covered by the passage of time. Which would be, today, among the many satellite cities, the latest Delhi? Gurgaon maybe?

A student of law, astronomy, philosophy, Sufism, logic, history, grammar, literature, Amir Khusrau was a poet of the Court, yet he always knew how to be at the very street level, and beyond castes or creeds. This admirable character is a whole model for today's India, which needs to look at the best of all its communities and not be reduced to a single religion or a monochromatic society.

Amir Khusrau is mostly famous for apparently having created the two musical instruments that best define Indian music—the sitar and the tabla. As if that were not enough, Ghazal and Khayal are two other basic styles of Hindustani music, from the north of the country, whose fatherhood is attributed to him, and at the same time, he is also considered as the father of qawwali, the sacred musical genre associated with the Sufi brotherhoods of the Indian subcontinent, based on singing, with harmonium and percussion accompaniment.

Among many other unforgettable festivals and religious festivities held in late evenings, I specially remember Ganesh Chaturthi. On one occasion, I had been invited by my good Indian friends, a couple, both publishers, to this important annual festival dedicated to Ganesha, the son of Shiva with the head of an elephant, so adored in India. He is considered to be auspicious for all enterprises that one wants to start, big or small. He is the one who inspires the beginning of something, whether material, intellectual, or spiritual, hence he is extremely dear to a wide range of Indians, from entrepreneurs to writers, to the most varied artists. I remember that night perfectly, as there had been numerous disturbances in New Delhi, as well as in Punjab and Haryana which had hampered our journey. Several people were killed and many injured after the Supreme Court of Justice condemned the guru, actor, and rock star, the Sikh Gurmeet Ram Rahim, for the rape, fifteen years ago, of two women linked to his followers, which brought him a twenty years" sentence, ten for each crime.

The grand festival of Ganesh Chaturthi, named thus after the fourth day of the month, had summoned a huge number of people on a sprawling property in the southeast of the capital, in an area known as Chhatarpur. It was an immense property belonging to a wealthy family, some of whose members I already knew, because of their friendship with Mr Sharma. Protected by a long and high wall from the outside as it was, one could not guess the interior of the farm house, euphemistically called so for the vast dimensions of the land, very much urban, of at least five hectares. When the massive metal gate opened, in front of the visitor's eyes they also opened a world unsuspected from the outside. Our car silently traversed the asphalt road next to the huge lawns of perfect and freshly cut grass, fountains that exhaled light blue illuminated water, and gleaming white marble Mughal pavilions. Completing everything, stood a temple erected majestically in the middle of the property, a small replica of a famous one from the south of the country dedicated to Shiva, with a Kailash Mountain, symbol of the abode of the great god. In the form of *char bagh* of the Mughal gardens, those pavilions, the rose garden, and subsequent parks, were something that seemed alien to what we had seen in the dirty and dark alleys, on our way. They seemed to belong to another country, something closer to the tourist brochures of five-star hotels, than to "real" India.

One could see three adjoining houses, in different styles, of the three brothers, That's something quite usual in families that made immense fortunes from the 70s with the sale of real estate for astronomical figures from the lands that their parents or grandparents had bought for almost nothing shortly after Independence. The jump into the interior from the streets surrounding the property, in effect, produced vertigo, as in a roller coaster. Finally, in silence, while these reflections passed through my mind, we arrived at one of those mansions, the last one. After greeting the children of the owners at the door, a young couple, friends of the one accompanying me, we went inside, where the Ganesh Chaturthi function was going to take place. The proportions inside the house were equally dazzling, especially for a European visitor, no matter how much, given my work, I was used to seeing large properties. There was a huge central room, typical of the reception of a large hotel in the capital. No less wide and tall, with a large dome in the centre and flowers arranged in tall glass vases on marble tables. Everything was in fact of enormous proportions, unthinkable for a family home anywhere else, how so ever rich the owner may be. Even a Sheikh of the Gulf or a Russian millionaire!

Something that caught my attention was that the decor was strikingly impersonal, empty and disappointing in some way for those dimensions and that fabulous setting, with a "standard" elegance similar to that of a hotel for tourist groups. Those distinguished gardens, the luxury of being able to enjoy a refreshing tranquillity and the sound of the water, deserved a more careful interior, rooted in the country's history, and equally exceptional in its detail. On the contrary, no furniture, painting, or detail revealed a personal touch. Yes! It was really strange! I thought that would happen only in the common areas, and then there would be personalized places, more intimate, warmer. But no! That was the tone of the whole property! The stairs, the dining room, the bar, and the different rooms. I entered a room a little later to use the washroom, and it turned out that there was nothing in there that denoted that a specific person lived there, with tastes and memories, with a touch of his own to show that this was their house. Yes! It had a pristine bathroom, with perfectly aligned towels, as in luxury hotels, or restaurants. Everything so standard! Everything so impersonal! It looked like a hotel suite! Correct, but cold.

After greeting part of the host family, we went to the altar at the end of the large space, on the right, with a representation of lord Ganesha in a life-size model of clay surrounded by lamps. It was the same idol that the next day would be immersed into the waters of the nearby Yamuna River, in a ceremony at dawn. A ceremony of the type less and less celebrated in big cities.

After the ritual offering to Ganesha, and having the pandit tie the thin red thread on our right wrist so it would bring us the best auspices, we sat down in grey armchairs, set in rows, in front of small tables with flowers. It never ceased to amaze me that this was a home, because by its dimensions it seemed like a theatre hall or convention centre. I wondered if the dozens, or hundreds of people, present that time, were not to be there, whether those who lived there would have the feeling of inhabiting a family space. Through the corridors, waiters were continually passing with soft drinks and non-alcoholic beverages, plus some spicy Indian snacks. My friends explained to me that this was obviously not for saving on costs, nor because the owners were abstainers, but because in religious festivities alcohol or any food that is not entirely vegetarian is not served. It was a real problem for me! At late hours of the evening, I cannot tolerate sweet juices, as they leave a bad taste in my mouth before dinner, and I always avoid them. After hesitating, I finally chose from the tray a tomato juice, in a long tulip glass, which in a vague way reminded me of a Bloody Mary. Fortunately it was salty, with pepper and some more spices, but obviously without vodka! I later changed my choice for a tonic with lemon and mint, which even more distantly suggested an exotic gin tonic. It was not a bad combination! Besides, the drinks were reasonably cold, something not easy to get in India, not even in select environments. Thus it was the whole evening, and then at dinner, alternating, first with pleasure, and then with patience, those two substitute delights.

As they did not stop circulating snacks, and time was passing while more and more people kept streaming in, I asked my companion if that was the dinner, spread over time, to which he smiled. "This is only finger food!" he said, pointing to a gate in the centre of the room, which lead to the garden. As I could see later, a large tent had been set up there, and a buffet with various types of food was arranged on elongated tables—Lebanese, Italian, Chinese, and of course Indian. We would still be there in the "imperial" room for a long time, as people would not stop coming in, after offering the customary greeting to the hosts at the monumental entrance. So the dinner did not start until well after ten. And the invitation was for 7.30 in the evening! We had arrived an hour late due to the traffic chaos caused by the disturbances of the actor guru. The truth is that I was not hungry, with the continuous appetizers. Nor did I want to extend my stay there indefinitely. Once one had met several people and covered the routine topics that can be spoken of in such circumstances, there comes a time when the forced blah-blah becomes tiresome, and I begin to have somewhat antisocial attitudes. What good are watches, I was wondering. Time here is the least of the worries! A thorough reflection on punctuality in India came upon me then. The point is that here it is considered low class to go straight to the food until a long ritual has been fulfilled, whereas in Europe it is the opposite! It would be considered bad etiquette to start the dinner almost three hours after the stipulated time.

India: A Unique Country in the World

To be yourself in a world that is constantly trying to make you something else is the greatest accomplishment.

Ralph Waldo Emerson

I began these memories and reflections in an endless traffic jam near the Gol Market, shortly after arriving in this city, five years ago.

And now as I am about to leave this beloved and feared country, the objective that brought me here, the house for Mr Sharma, having been accomplished I am reminded of that difficult beginning since the same situation has emerged again. It happened with another driver, Ashwin, calmer and more educated than his predecessor, and yet my experience with him has been identical. In addition to doing something quite similar with the heater, he insists on accelerating heavily, and builds up incredible speed, sometimes going faster in second gear than in fourth. What happens is that, he puts the car into the first, then the second, accelerates to the maximum, and the whole vehicle vibrates as if it were an airplane about to take off, and then he slams the the brakes within a few metres. Quick acceleration and sudden braking! Those seem to be the only two aspects of driving a car that he knows. It's bizarre!

I tell myself that it's strange he doesn't think, at his sixty odd years, that continuity and fluidity are more beneficial in the short and long term, than the extremes of start and stop. Also, what sense does it make to step on the accelerator when you know that you have to brake in a few metres for a crossing, or a traffic light? But no! He bears down on the accelerator pedal hard as if by instinct. What happens afterwards, we'll see later! My thoughts at that moment were exactly the same as the ones in that endless traffic jam near Gol Market. There it was the temperature control, here it is speed. Can't this man maintain the speed in an intermediate zone? That way we would be able to travel in a comfortable relaxed manner, without jerks and jolts. Well, no! And if I say anything to him, he clams up. It has happened on several occasions, so I prefer to keep quiet.

Since those early days, there has been a noticeable transformation in me, a great change in my personal situation. From a certain point onwards, I knew that everything would change for the better, even though I was not able to foresee how long I would be in Delhi, assuming all the difficulties and contradictions encountered in daily life. Though all of those were resolved in the end. What was clear was that all that was happening, was definitely positive. There was a sense of continually discovering new keys within me and in the country itself, after the first labyrinthine period. As if by magic, the most toxic characters of the early days were changing dramatically into close and warm friends, not many in number, but enough. Seen in perspective, a labyrinth always has, like so many other things, three parts or phases. One is at the entrance, usually with a winding path that must be followed with eyes wide open, and which leads to the centre, inexorably to the core of all problems to treasure. It is here that the confrontation with the enemy takes place, be it a Minotaur, or a beast. Or more often with ourselves! Hence one of the most important symbols linked to Daedalus is the double bladed axe or the labrys, to simultaneously open the way out and in. It is the site of the struggle, that brings clarity and awakening, either with the victory or the end of the opponent. The third phase, of coming to life, of keeping the "hero" alive and letting him regain his orientation, consists of getting out of the maze, which in most cases is quite not easy, and enormously long—like one of the worst nightmares. Absolute self-confidence is required, but even that is not enough. It is also necessary to have something or someone outside, on the other side of the walls, which is worth fighting for and going out to—love, projects, and goals. This phase is a fabulous and unpredictable mix of what is internal, and what is external to oneself. Without aspiring to find meaning in this struggle, the sense of it, one can never come out!

Only later did the true objective of my sojourn in India become clearer. I had come here for something greater, something more far-reaching and ambitious than merely building a house in New Delhi. All the elements and the steps, however, since my departure from Spain till the conclusion of the work, sometimes fast, at others extremely slow, were necessary and played an indispensable, precise role. That is how it was, from the harsh settling down on arrival, and the progression to new situations and opportunities that my work and the country offered me, to a state of near happiness in recent years, with numerous trips and discoveries throughout India.

Time went by… From the first months to the subsequent four years. Such was the long and fruitful period of the construction of Mr Sharma's house! As always, the project in the quiet and elegant Chanakyapuri neighbourhood took much longer than anticipated due to the elaboration of the plans, the calculations, the permits, the search for appropriate materials and other necessary supplies. Most of the times, projects do not end when we decide they will end. Rather, it is what we do that mysteriously arranges their resolution.

From the beginning, the owner had been very pleased with my proposed idea of a large villa with marked similarities to the old Roman and Pompeian houses. I wanted an ambience with some local Indian influences, but above all I desired a Mediterranean air to prevail—blue, warm, open, and bright, closer to what is found in Goa, Kerala, and the west coast, than in New Delhi or the big Indian cities. In these Roman patrician villas, a central patio already existed since Greek and Etruscan times in the Mediterranean and a good part of life revolved around a courtyard, impluvium, in the centre of which is a small rectangular pool to collect rainwater. At the top of the complex was the *compluvium*, which consisted of a central opening in the ceiling, which allowed sunlight to penetrate into the small or large cloister, illuminating the rooms on all four sides of the house. In this way, the entire interior of the structure was filled with natural, overhead light, constantly distributing its benefits. Light, health, and well-being were always synonymous for me! Another Mediterranean element, also present in India, is the roof, the flat roof, which crowned and closed the building.

The building under construction, with four practically identical facades, differing only in the number and shape of the windows, has certain similarities with the famous Rotonda by the Renaissance architect Andrea Palladio, near Venice in northern Italy. The square floor plan is symmetrical, as in the Rotonda, except that the central hall is not circular, but square. All the rooms are also rectangular, and arranged around a central hall, having generous views from both inside and outside, of the surroundings. The building has two very large floors. The upper one is basically dedicated to bedrooms, dressing rooms, family living rooms, with various "view points" into the garden. On the lower level are the reception and celebration rooms, the dining room, the library, and the office. The set has nine square blocks, or cubes, a precise and odd number that makes it possible to have an empty space at its core.

The basic idea of the structure, in which I invested several of the best years of my life, not without difficulties, was to create an axis of light in the centre of the building, which as per the image I had of it from the beginning, it had to be square. A big square with nine blocks, three on each side. This open space in the centre of the glass-enclosed courtyard is akin to what in ancient Indian architecture is called *Brahmasthana*, the "place of the spirit", the vacant space in the holiest part of the Hindu temple. In the Hindu tradition, such a place acts, as a kind of invocation to prosperity and divine inspiration for the one who is there. It is the true nucleus, the imaginary axis on which the building rotates!

To carry out my work, and in the field of documentation, I concentrated on the projects of three renowned architects, whose works are emblematic in India—Le Corbusier, Doshi and Correa. Le Corbusier (1877–1965) came to India in the early fifties with the arduous task of delineating a model city, the future Chandigarh, destined to represent the new and hopeful phase that India began to live after Independence. The work had been entrusted to him by the brand new Prime Minister, Jawaharlal Nehru, a mixture of British practicality and Indian tenacity, as well as a few drops of intelligent dandyism added to the elaborate cocktail. In such an extremely traditional country, it was to symbolize everything that 20th century modernity entailed, which India was trying to integrate and catch up with, after the painful separation with Pakistan. Lahore, the historical capital of Punjab, would remain on the other side and its place would be taken by the new city of Chandigarh, where the sadness of the more than traumatic separation would become the hope of an enduring future. Also, from 1966, it would be the capital of Punjab, and shared with neighbouring Haryana. The emphasis of the project was on rational planning in urbanization and in the buildings themselves, since in theory it was to be a sort of model for the capitals of the emerging Indian states. However, except in the case of Bhubaneshwar, in Odisha, it was hardly followed by any other of the congested cities of the country, so young and at the same time so old.

Charles Édouard Jeanneret-Gris, known since 1950 as Le Corbusier, had the virtue of projecting buildings that perfectly incorporated each of their elements, so that as set pieces, they seemed more like the work of a Swiss watchmaker than of an architect. He was, indeed, born in the Swiss canton of Neuchâtel! It was not by chance either, that his profession during his youth had been that of a watchmaker, which is corroborated by the commitment and meticulousness that this master imprinted in his built works, and in all his projects. Designer of furniture and objects, as well as an urban planner and painter, along with Frank Lloyd Wright, or Ludwig Mies van der Rohe, Le Corbusier is considered one of the supreme examples of modern architecture. His paradigm and influence undoubtedly extended to various fields throughout the second half of the 20th century. Not surprisingly, the justification given by the United Nations Educational, Scientific, and Cultural Organization (UNESCO), when declaring the work of Le Corbusier in Chandigarh, especially the Capitol complex as World Heritage was that he had invented "a new architectural language".

Something that is often heard, between serious reflection and joke, is that this "new" capital of Punjab does not seem like an Indian city. And indeed, it doesn't. In addition to its "rationality", the strict parallel and perpendicular lines of its arteries, it is the one that registers the highest number of cars per inhabitant, because without one's own means or without public transport, it is impossible to cover its long distances on foot. What this half joke, serious at heart, carries within itself is the somewhat rhetorical question whether every city in this country needs chaos, extreme noise, and unpredictable commotion to be considered Indian.

Chandigarh's order is indeed unusual in the context of the subcontinent, and seems to be inspired by the hopscotch game, as well as the human body, which was a decisive moderating factor for Le Corbusier. After the European absolutisms of World War II, in which the model was mastodontic and impersonal, the Swiss architect proposed in his book *The Modulor*, a new order closer to the human scale and the golden ratio. According to this comparison with the standard size of the human body, the divisions of the city would have a parallel with the organism—the digestive system would be directly related to the industrial and workshop area, the circulatory with the seven arterial roads that cross the city, and the heart with the nerve centre of the city, the lungs being its green areas with scattered groves. In the Capitol, which hosts the regional Parliament, are the three most important buildings that the Swiss architect built—the Supreme Court (judiciary), the Assembly (legislative branch) and the Secretariat (executive branch). Montesquieu's spirit of separation of powers, which offers and entails democratic modernity, was thus well served to act as a starting point for the "new" India of the 50s. The initial plan consisted of about fifty identical rectangles (a kilometre long on average), linked by long roads, which in turn were constituted in neighbourhoods with a certain autonomy of shops, hospitals, schools, and temples. As always, theory is one thing and practice another!

Le Corbusier worked intensively on this layout from 1951 until his death in 1965. He was helped by a team of close collaborators, starting with his own wife, and about twenty young Indian architects, among whom the young Balkrishna Doshi (Pune, India, 1927) stood out. Doshi, current dean of the architects of this Asian country, had travelled to Paris when he was 24 years old, and worked there for five years with Le Corbusier. He communicated with him in the limited English that the teacher knew, about which he would comment later with mirth that "when a language is not mastered, everything is done in the most spatial and visual conversation."

This great creator, Balkrishna Doshi interested in integrating architecture, urban planning, and landscaping into a fluid whole, recently won the Pritzker Prize, and has a hundred top-order buildings distributed throughout much of India, especially Ahmedabad, where he resides. Among his works is Kamala House (1958), his own home, wherein he plays with natural light which enters, in a studied manner, the interior in different planes. Among many other works in the capital of Gujarat, and he is the author of quite a few, are the

Central Bank, the Tagore Hall, or the Institute of Indology. One of Doshi's most representative approaches can be seen in the Tagore Theatre (1967), in which he tries to give a "local" response, not an imported one, to the massive use of concrete, present in most of its constructions. Many of Doshi's structures have a premeditated and widespread use of load-bearing walls with this material which defines the 20th century, in order to achieve a thermal mattress against the extremely warm and oppressive weather of this Asian country.

Besides his architectural training, Balkrishna Doshi has a clear social interest, and is enrolled in a group of professionals who declare themselves workers in the service of society. One of the clearest examples of this was the Aranya project in Indore (1989), based on the generalization of common spaces at low cost, consisting of a series of homes with internal courtyards, which provide accommodation for several thousands from very low income families. That is why Doshi won the Aga Khan Architecture Award in 1993–1995. In Chandigarh, together with Le Corbusier, he had the important role of projecting homes for thousands of middle level state employees. This gave way to his continued interest in creating the best community spaces, simple and low cost. The Gandhi Smarak Sangrahalaya, in Ahmedabad (1958–1963), is another of his best-known projects, and constitutes an important monument dedicated to the great Indian leader of the 20th century, Mahatma Gandhi.

Although naturally influenced by renowned international figures of 20th-century architecture, as with his compatriot, the late Charles Correa, Doshi never copies, rather he carries out an assimilation of many elements, his own and foreign. Both great contemporary creators reaffirmed their roots through their works, shortly after the country achieved independence from the British Empire.

Considered as the "greatest architect of contemporary India", Charles Correa, was an urbanist and architecture theorist. No one embodies like he does, local, native art, and style, perfectly materializing that contemporary saying about thinking globally, but knowing how to act locally. Born in Hyderabad in 1930, an urban planner and architecture theorist, Charles Mark Correa studied in the US, at the University of Michigan and the Massachusetts Institute of Technology, and his greatest contribution is the recovery of non-Western patterns for modernity. As in the case of his contemporaries Achyut Kanvinde, or Raj Rewal, his maximum contribution is to propose that modernity and tradition are not opposing elements or thoughts, but complementary in multiple paths, many yet to be explored. As in several other domains, the 20th century historically was a kind of privileged balcony from which to look at the rest of the times. There had never been so much information and progress in human civilization in such a short space of time. Correa, like Doshi and the other architects, located in the immense context of this subcontinent with such diversity, knew how to investigate their own as well as older patterns. The idea was clear—architecture should be one of the protagonists of change. As had happened in other Asian countries such as Iraq or Egypt, here too after Independence, with Jawaharlal Nehru as Indian Prime Minister, architecture became one of the instruments of renewal, and attempted to create a new national identity.

One of the most characteristic works of Correa is the National Museum of Crafts, New Delhi (1975–1990), which displays the dialogue maintained between the open buildings and their relationship with the courtyards and spaces that surround them. The relationship of the intense light of the sun with the shadows, and the use of local materials, considered humble, are other hallmarks of his projects. His legacy includes, besides the Gandhi Memorial in Gujarat, Bharat Bhavan and Vidhan Bhavan, in Bhopal, and the British Council of New Delhi, as also the Kala Academy in Goa.

For all this, he was awarded the Padma Shri in 1972 and the Padma Vibhushan in 2006, one of the top awards in India.

Charles Correa, though deeply rooted in India has an unmistakeable cosmopolitan air, and is able to combine the Indianness with modernity and offer an architecture of great universal interest. Spaces open to the sky and the environment may be considered one of the hallmarks of many of his projects, such as the unrealized one for the pavilion of India, in Osaka, Japan (1969), Bharat Bhavan (1975–1981) and Vidhan Bhavan (1980–1986), both in Bhopal. Sadly, the so-called New Bombay, which was destined to accommodate two million people, remained on paper, and was never built.

Like all modalities of art in India, architecture constitutes a grand metaphor, an excellent and joyful occasion to uncover the mystery and the Absolute of the cosmos in the concreteness of visible and palpable walls and spaces. At the same time, and thanks to a circle in constant rotation, the concreteness is expressed in the Absolute. Be it a painting, a cave, a sculpture or the structure of a temple, this flow of opposite mirrors, between near and far, is achieved through certain shapes and dimensions, with certain materials and orientations, creating a bridge, as would hardly be found in other places, between the finite and the infinite, between the mundane, palpable reality, and the eternal, mystical one.

The *Vastu Shastra*, as the classical science of architecture is called in India, is contained in various treatises written in Sanskrit on how the temples and buildings ought to be, even in their minutest details. The word “shastra” can be translated as teaching or doctrine, which together becomes something like the “science of inhabiting”. It is a conglomerate of very diverse fields, which include elements such as the basic drawing of the building, its measurements, the implicit and explicit geometric scheme, as well as the arrangement of the ground and the space around. One of the most famous works is the *Shilpa Prakasha*, written in Odisha in the 10th century. It describes and lays down all the geometric details of the Hindu sanctuaries, linking them to the symbolism of the human body, both in its form and its emotions—drama, passion and recollection. The chapters of these works include not only the varied architectural elements of temples, but also of houses and cities, of fortifications and engineering works, related to water, or communications, as well as the canalization of rivers, and public toilets. In the early 1950s, Le Cobusier incorporated some of the principles of *Vastu Shastra* into Chandigarh, the new capital of Punjab.

In brief, one can affirm that the basis of temple architecture is a mandala, a symbolic representation of the cosmos, which always has the *bindu* as its centre, the circular stroke, or "drop", which is traditionally considered the origin of Creation. This represents, both in the symbolic and material plane, the unity of the Being before the expansion of the universe, as well as its subsequent withdrawal in the "Night of Brahma". During this, everything visible is hidden for a long time before a new expansion can happen in a cycle, without beginning or end. Around this navel, from which everything comes, and which a contemporary scientist would identify with the atom prior to the Big Bang, symmetric structures are chained in concentric layers, which end up conforming the building. In short, and with a spiritual and ritual significance in the three main religions of India—Jainism, Buddhism, and Hinduism, it all comes down to the relationship of the circle with the square in successive series, the first being the representation of the cosmos and the second of the Earth. The overlapping of one with the other, conjugated with triangles, symbols, and representations, ends up constituting the mandala, the geometric and schematic representation of the whole.

The most important mandala is the Manduka Mandala, with the same number of squares as the chess board, 64 (8 x 8) squares or nakshatras, and the Paramasaayika Mandala, of 82 squares. In the Vastu Purusha, the Manduka Mandala is drawn with an anthropomorphic figure, with the head towards the Northeast and feet towards the Southwest.

Ever since I began acquainting myself with ancient Indian architecture in order to apply it to my budding house project, what interested me immensely was that in the central area of all the mandalas was an element known as *Brahmasthana*, the "place of spirit". It is a void, a wide hollow in the most sacred part of the temple, which seeks prosperity and divine inspiration. That empty centre of the house is like a nucleus that bears fruit towards the outer sides. Along with making everything that is around breathe, it introduces a fascinating counterpoint between the nuclear and the accessory on being applied to the structure, between the axis and the rotating ends of the building. I was fascinated by this constituent element of traditional Indian architecture, which is defined by absence, and which, certainly, was a great influence in designing the villa at Chanakyapuri, commissioned by the owner in that distant December of 2013. The owner found it magnificent. In several meetings prior to the completion of the project, I pointed out to Mr Sharma how important it is to include this element in the building, a bit in the manner of an Andalusian patio or Roman impluvium, so that such vacant space would give light to the house from the inside, creating a kind of axis of light in all the rooms spread over the two floors.

During its long presence in the Indian Subcontinent, the British Raj was not interested in the traditional architecture of India, the *Vastu Vidya*, but rather took Islamic and Mughal models, in what was called the Indo-Saracenic style, typical of the Victorian era, especially in Madras and Mumbai. It has large domes and pointed arches, all fortified with a structure of great solidity, built mostly of limestone.

Except for the construction of modern temples such as Akshardham, in the capital, or a rare researcher or Sanskritist, no one wanted to explore the possibilities of *Sastra Vidya* in colonial constructions, because it seemed archaic. Perhaps the study of *Sastra Vidya* was relegated to the background in the syllabus of schools of architecture, since it was far from the priorities of the expected projects in their upcoming careers. Indeed, although Indian architects are aware that if they applied the principles of *Sastra Vidya* their inhabitants would gain in health and well-being, it must be recognized that they hardly take the trouble to rescue such patriotic traditions. Because of that, a minimalist aesthetic now reigns, with paradoxical Baroque touches, perhaps arising from the socialist stage, due to close proximity with the Soviet orbit.

Among the social activities that I attended in the evenings, several were book launches. One of them was a curious and instructive afternoon in the Longchamp Hall of the Hotel Taj Man Singh. The event was going to take place in the big room on the topmost floor of the hotel, very close to my house where I often went to eat at its Chinese restaurant, one of the best in the city. This time it was not for a dinner with chopsticks, but for the launch of the latest novel by a well-known editor of the *Hindustan Times*. Although the time mentioned in the invitation was at 7 pm, contrary to my habit, I did not arrive on time, because nobody here does. It's a kind of unwritten rule. It never occurs to anyone to get there "on the dot", least of all for such social events where they are quite lax with the time. The later, the better! You can thus give the impression of being very busy! On the other hand, I did not want to present myself after an excessive delay and maybe lose a thoughtful, or funny introduction, or both. Besides, although it was a novel, the subject of the book, ancient Indian history, interested me greatly. Apparently, the novel was about Ashoka, the last sovereign of the Maurya dynasty and almost a contemporary of Alexander the Great. He very intelligently converted his kingdom to Buddhism, after being convinced that such a religion was the best for his people and for himself.

As mythical a figure as can be, Ashoka was the third emperor of the Maurya, a short but brilliant dynasty that dominated much of the subcontinent, including present day Pakistan and Afghanistan, between the 4th and 2nd centuries BC. In addition to other surprising features, this court had a Greek ambassador, Megasthenes, who made known in the West, the wonders of India, like the existence of yogis, the gymnosophists, who lived naked in the woods, in deep meditation, among many others. The turning point of his reign was when appalled by the devastation and death that his brutal conquest of the kingdom of Kalinga (Odisha) had caused, he turned to Buddhism in repentance, and abjured the use of violence as a means of governance. Ruling with renewed ethics, which brought a period of great wealth to the country, he extended the empire from the capital Pataliputra (now Patna) over the Gangetic plain, unifying for the first time in history, a good part of the territory of present day India. Symbols of remembrance of that transcendent moment remain, such as the Capital of Ashoka. This sculpture, found in Sarnath, has four lions with their backs together on a circular base with other animals, and was adopted as the official emblem of India in 1950. In addition to this, there are the pillars of Ashoka, famous stone columns with inscriptions of Buddhist and legal texts, scattered throughout the north of the country. About 12 metres high, and weighing up to 50 tons, these pillars were located in other landmark places of Buddha's life. Of them some twenty have survived.

Numerous thoughts on this fruitful period crossed my mind as I arrived at the Taj Man Singh, about twenty or twenty-five minutes late. Up there, however, there was practically no one, just three or four people, who must surely have been old friends, as they talked animatedly in a closed circle. Fortunately, the sponsor of the event was a well-known brand of Scotch whiskey, which was served generously by numerous waiters and at the bar, in small pegs, with or without ice. One could drink as much as one wanted, something not very usual in India. In fact, it was totally unusual since that liquid gold so coveted, is yet prohibited in some states. About 15 minutes after getting there, as I made time with the drink and the wide landscape that stretched down below the windows, several people began to arrive, looking relaxed and talkative. Among them was the friend who had sent me the invitation, a Spaniard who had been residing in New Delhi for a long time, and who treasured an extensive knowledge of Indian society. While I was talking with her and some other guests, who clearly she had known for a long time, the writer of renown entered, and when he came to our circle he was introduced to me. Young and very smiling, dressed in black and white. I tried to chat with him, say something about Ashoka and the interesting Mauryan Empire, although I sensed that he did not want to go too deep into those moments in the historical character. Maybe it was not the occasion I thought.

From what I had read, I was very attracted to this period of great change, in which after being a fierce warrior, the emperor converted to Buddhist peace, invited yogis and sages to his court in order to have deep religious and philosophical debates with them, something similar to how two thousand years later the other great emperor, Akbar, would do in Fatehpuri Sikri. No wonder they have perhaps been the two richest and most flourishing periods of Indian history, the summits of the great Maurya and Mughal empires, when the maximum power at the top fomented a dialogue not merely of form among cultures and religions but also content. In the case of Ashoka the agglutinant for the very first time, was Buddhism, the Indian religion which, next to Jainism, seems to be the one that most poorly weds power, and all mechanisms linked to it, by demanding one to rid oneself of desire, and try not to inflict evil on others, and seek the straight path… He was very much that King philosopher who would have delighted Plato, from little more than a century earlier. Ashoka had taken a big step, difficult, and firm, following in the footsteps of the Buddha himself. For this, he left on a nine month pilgrimage to Sarnath, near Benares, where the Enlightened One had given his first sermon on the Four Noble Truths, about the suffering that afflicts existence, that would change humanity. From there Ashoka left for Bodh Gaya, the town in Vihar where under the Bodhi tree, Prince Siddartha Gautam achieved illumination, thus becoming, one dawn, the Enlightened One.

Moved by the history of the creator of this religion, who walked away from the security of his palace to enlightenment through extreme asceticism, and the discovery of an intermediate way, the emperor erected in that place a great temple, which exists to this day. From that moment on, he was called *Dharma Ashoka*, or "the pious Ashoka". After his conversion to Buddhism, the emperor founded numerous stupas and shrines containing the relics of Buddha, throughout Southeast Asia.

I was in these reflections and memories of my readings, when, a good while later, about half past eight, I went back to speak with the author, and trying to be nice, not to seem too inquisitive, I asked him about when he expected the announced presentation to begin. A kind of stage had been planned for that, with a microphone and several posters depicting the cover of the newly published book. With some surprise at my insistent interest, the writer replied that "that is the least important thing". After seeing the astonishment on my face, and maybe to reduce the tension, he added, "The important thing is to meet with friends and see each other!" Time was passing! I entertained myself with the huge panoramic views of the entire city from the top floor of that large building, between the great ceremonial avenue Raj Path and the commercial area of Connaught Place. Night had fallen some time ago, and thousands of red lights of the tiny cars were moving slowly down there, circulating as they could along the roundabouts and main arteries of the city near Jan Path. Fortunately, in a nearby huddle there were some attractive women with whom I chatted for a while, especially a mother and her daughter, with very similar faces. And a little further, I stopped again in the circle of my friend, exchanging some words with other people who were introduced to me. Among them, I met several characters, a businessman and also a photographer, who had just published a book about tea in India, a magnificent coffee table book that he would generously send me days later, when I expressed my desire to have it. I commented that I had been fascinated by the tea plantations of Himachal Pradesh, next to the Kangra Valley and in Palampur, much more than the famous ones of Darjeeling. The tea gardens of Himachal are very special places, where you can breathe and perceive something beyond time and space, where energies flow unique to the low foothills of the Himalayas.

A little later, I happened to also chat with a film director who had just made a documentary about the Himalayas. We talked about Ladakh, the region north of Kashmir, also called Little Tibet, one of my favorite places in India. I had visited innumerable Buddhist temples in distant hills, in isolated places. In every temple we entered, many of them closed, it was a revelation—the prayer room charged with an indefinable primeval energy, and the great statue of the Maitreya Buddha, the Buddha of the Future, usually presiding over it.

The truth is that those conversations were unexpectedly pleasant, enriching, and thanks to them I did not lose an evening. But my mind at that moment was focused on Ashoka. Yes! Everything was fantastic, but time was passing inexorably by, and no one made the slightest gesture of approaching the stage to start the announced introduction of the book. At that late hour, I only felt the whiskeys beginning to crowd in my head! Exhausted from the innumerable comments left mid-way, as is usually done on these occasions, it being already past nine, two hours after the announced launch, I finally decided to leave to get some rest. I had woken up at seven in the morning and had worked non stop all day! That was the apology to myself! But I really felt quite tired at the end of the day. Still, surprised by the delay I communicated to my friend with signs that I was retiring. She merely smiled. Obviously, she knew the new Indian society much better than I did!

I never did get to know if that presentation actually happened! Therefore, it can be said that it was the launch of a book without its presentation!

A good number of Indians, including Brahmins and Kshatriyas, have now become global merchants in "public relations" of a borderless market. Also some gurus, such as Sri Sri Ravi Shankar, who did not want to be left behind in the great race, have become parallel businessmen. A large number of Maharajas are similarly rushing to become creators of hotel brands, through the restoration of their ancestral palaces and pavilions. This qualitative change in the use of such properties is presented as a "heritage home" experience, as a "hidden gem" which can be found by tourists pleasurable, as described by one of the owners. "A paradise between yesterday, today and tomorrow." In short, the message is that the "magic world" of the royals can be experienced by anyone who can afford it.

It is true that Independence from the British Empire meant a violent change in the lives of the sovereigns of small and large states, with many of their privileges suddenly withdrawn, though not their titles, which were also about to be annulled in a close parliamentary vote. It is interesting in this regard to read today the *Mandala*, an illuminating and almost unknown book, written by a Nobel Prize for Literature winner, already forgotten by the new generations—Pearl S. Buck. Throughout the narrative, of enormous descriptive richness and great narrative fluency, one can see how the Maharaja of Udaipur, father of the current Arvind Singh, suggests for the first time immediately after Independence, that his summer palace in the middle of Lake Pichola, be turned into a distinguished hotel. This is the same exceptional aquatic enclave that in the future would be known as Lake Palace, a point of attraction for many rich tourists who visit this historic city of Rajasthan throughout the year, the likes of whom can hardly be seen in other places, except for some privileged establishment in Kochi or Jaipur. For this, after the hopeful, though traumatic date of 1947, Maharana Bhagwant Singh Mewar brought an American architect to carry out the restoration work of the complex project. The memories and reflections of the Maharaja upon waking up one morning, and the relationship of love and forced distancing from his properties, until then of almost divine origin, together with the link with his wife, help one visualize in this interesting, almost biographical novel, to what extent India changed in a few years. It transitioned in this brief period, from a quasi-feudal era, from wars and unimaginable extravagances of the royalty, to have to compete with the sharpest weapon of the 20th century—money! The cool, elusive and fluid money!

Many of the Maharajas had to convert per force into businessmen. Those who had ruled their states for generations without opposition or a greater justification than power gained through battles, also had to enter into the political battlefield in some places, becoming democratically elected leaders. They were "passionate about restoring their heritage". But the truth was that they aspired for a Rolex watch or an Armani bag!

Even today, mainly in Rajasthan, ever so often it comes to the public and the press that the dilapidated palace of this or that princely state is being turned into a hotel, not just any hotel, but a "heritage hotel". Presented in advertisements as the "paradise of hospitality", it is suggested to the potential client that he can live a few days in a unique location, as a royal guest, with all experiences, just short of hunting tigers in a gleaming Rolls Royce. At some of the hotels, he is fabulously received by a trumpeter and his entourage, as in the grand Umaid Bhawan Palace, in Jodhpur. The online or print promotion presents the hotels as though "the Maharajas have opened their palaces", where one can have experiences from times gone by, with hunts, intimate concerts, and unique service, all to feel "like the guests of a king". From extremely elitist and expensive establishments such as the Ram Bagh of Jaipur, or the Oberoi Amarvilas of Agra, there is a wide range of palatial enclaves converted into hotels, some of which are quiet and discreet places, such as the Ahilya Fort from Maheshwar, facing the unusually clean legendary Narmada River.

The idea that underlies this activity, "forced" on many occasions, is beneficial and even brilliant, since it solves several problems in one go, rescuing the heritage buildings from destruction and oblivion, and granting them a new life. They also contribute to revitalizing a region of the country through domestic and foreign tourism.

The reality, however, is not so rosy. The truth is that for now, these private initiatives, although very interesting and applauded, are like tiny isolated worlds which have little to do with the surrounding population, being for the exclusive benefit of the owner and his closest family. Given this unusual wealth of the new billionaires, it is unfortunate that there are really few cases of altruism and social responsibility projects by extremely wealthy entrepreneurs. There are hardly any hospitals, may be some trusts, with negligible activity, which given their numbers makes them practically non-existent in the enormity of the subcontinent.

The age of "Make In India" slogan launched a few years ago by the current Prime Minister, has unfortunately had a dry harvest, because it has not yet brought to light any significant product. The reason for this is the scant investment in improving the quality of materials and processing as well as the problem of unskilled labour, since there is no educational policy on the teaching of trades. The booming sectors such as pharmaceuticals and handicrafts for the tourism sector are an exception. Everything that comes from the traditional world, backed by centuries of continuity and strong roots, needs to be actively promoted. There is no shortage of wonderful raw materials in India, from those used in textiles to construction materials, wood, minerals and others, but it is the zero investment in processing that makes the products obsolete, and old, often even before they are launched.

Indeed, there is not even an isolated case of an attempt to rescue lost trades, or those in decline. Yes, there is much to be done, like aid to students, with scholarships in various fields that foster creativity and entrepreneurship in sectors close to the needs of the people. For example in diverse trades, classical music, art, and so many others fields, donations to help orphans and poor girls would go long way. Except for some rare cases like the Transparency International India Rajasthan Chapter (Coalition against Corruption), the phenomenon is often the reverse. More and more machines are replacing labour, including in traditional Indian sectors, such as weaving, where electric looms have been introduced for making silk for saris.

As a pretext, the wealthy families of real or supposed ancestry sometimes affirm that "We must remember our past, but not dwell in past glories." When that is precisely what they would love to do, live in a disproportionately privileged situation with respect to the rest of their fellow citizens. Some have managed to do so thanks to the properties they still own, and from which they can obtain benefits, with sales or rentals. Others have been forced to become businessmen to obtain liquid and palpable money.

Young men engaged in various businesses, like to describe themselves as "luxury car fanatic", or "eccentric" and "passionate". While women do so with this last qualifier, "passionate", or as "familial" and "perfectionist". They declare as the most normal thing in the world that "I want to have my own plane!" And of course, it is not a small plane, but a powerful jet in which to go to London or Dubai for business, or Bali and the Seychelles for a vacation. Perhaps they have read about the eccentricities carried out as a norm by the Maharajas of not-so-distant times, condemned to a golden boredom. And they want to resemble them! Many are also secretly fascinated with the case of China, due to the economic acceleration that this neighbouring giant experienced in recent years, and which has earned it the second place on the planet, already in competition with the eternal first in the ranking, the USA. In 1960, the per capita income of China was the same as India's. Today, that of China is five times higher.

These new rich, who enjoy clothes, products, and properties unthinkable for the vast majority of Indians, feel heady about things like going to Monte Carlo, or Dubai, just for the purpose of eating and shopping over a weekend. Of the "Old Europe", except the

Mediterranean coast for a short vacation, nothing attracts them except London, the great metropolis of other times, although eaten today by the doubts of Brexit. Minimalism doesn't seem to have entered their extravagant lifestyle which it did for example in architecture.

Unlike in the West, where there occurred a rapid and frank decline of the patriarchal model, which became the consequence and origin of so many social crises, India seems to be immunized against them. Here, there remains a great admiration for the father figure, encrypted in discipline and ambition in equal measure. Indeed, perhaps as a sign of natural intelligence based on survival, continuity is vital, and the basic cell of traditional society—the family, has not been destroyed. Its constant support and presence are essential for any life project! Every culture aspires, without a doubt, to have its key of sustenance through the vicissitudes of time, that central stone, which if removed from the entrance arch would bring down the entire building. In this case, it is the family.

At present in India, there are basically two models of potentate, of the individual who is supposed to cause envy and admiration wherever he goes. One of these models is that of the young high-tech technocrat entrepreneur, with wide international connections, in the style of the creators of Apple, Steve Jobs, "the man who changed the world", or Facebook, Mark Elliot Zuckerberg, who the *Vanity Fair* magazine placed at the top of the most influential people in the world. And what specially works is the model of Elon Musk, investor and South African tycoon with Canadian and American nationality, founder among others of Tesla, in addition to being co-founder of PayPal, SpaceX, Hyperloop, SolarCity, among others. Such icons are always the most admired here! And along with them, they are passionate about all those firms, so concrete and so unbelievable at the same time, based not on palpable objects, but on social networks, advertising and information, such as Google or Facebook, with resonances in marketing, design, and latest technology. These are the ones that fascinate them, and constitute the top of their interests.

The other type of new rich which hundreds of thousands, or millions of young Indians aspire to be, is the Russian, who overwhelms the four cardinal points of the globe without having anyone as a model. He only has a mirror to look at himself, because wherever he goes, with the great capital he has just amassed, he seems so free of complexes, so free of any history other than that of his meteoric rise. This is precisely where the currently popular term "oligarch" comes from, from the Greek "Óligós", meaning the few; it actually implies a degeneration of the idea of aristocracy as "the power of the best", given that it no longer possesses noble aspirations nor the accumulated virtues of distinction and discipline. They neither have these qualities nor do they claim to have them, because such oligarchs are only interested in spending money in abundance, and above all appearing to be doing it, in order to satisfy a constant need to stand out from the rest as winners. They are not worried that this is a poor way to raise their own self-esteem, or that it is a sad model to offer to the society, based on something as fragile and changing as relying solely on what one possesses, not on what one is. Many of these characters love to talk about themselves in the third person, thus placing themselves beyond the common mortals, who have to fight not only to maintain their personal and family situation, but to create it.

Unfortunately, this model, unsupportive of the rest, and forged in iron, is reaching the new rich of the entire Earth, placed as they are beyond any ethics, any social or human principles. Although it is, as in the Chinese case, in open contradiction with the theoretical political regime. But that does not matter! All paradoxes are assumed by the logic of economic superiority. The grotesque and the caricaturesque part is that this, surprisingly, is now the trend, simply in order to become famous. The cultural and aesthetic degradation that we have witnessed in recent decades by those who have local or world trade in their hands, is perceived on a large scale in a swift banalization, by virtue of which the current "influencers", and "socialites" are who they are. Fascinated with the easy vertigo offered by new communications, competitive sport, fashion, business relocations, constant changes of place, it seems that they would like to imitate God—be everywhere and be nowhere.

In this world of new designers, flooded with "creative artists" with "magnetic personalities", young men and women, especially from well-to-do families, aspire to become nothing other than fashion designers, couturiers, furniture artists and interior designers. Although it must be said that this is a world-wide phenomenon! Everyone wants today their 15 minutes of international fame! The main mantra is no longer Om for a collective of millions of people! On the contrary, now it seems to be, "I am busy", or "he is very busy". The coolest thing is to have a "very busy agenda". If this happens, it is because the important thing, perhaps the only important thing in today's globalized society, is to give the impression of having succeeded. The danger is that many meteoric ascents are followed by equally meteoric falls. It is such a fragile and changing world! All this seems to be happening under an intense wave of "Americanization" in the values of life, although this phenomenon would be considered contradictory here, happening within a very traditional social system. The risk facing this country, due to the vertiginous economic changes of recent years, is that the extreme differentiation between the bouquet of millionaires or billionaires, and the immeasurable field of the forgotten, and the disinherited, is consolidated and eternalized. The danger of falling apart in a few generations is real, so that in a short time India as we know it may have disappeared.Ancient India, turned into a caricature of itself.

Luxury does not only consist of large and expensive mansions, of long and overwhelming cars, or clothes of iconic brands in which the first thing that stands out is the price. No! Real luxury is what cannot be bought with money alone! Elegance comes not from one's capacity to pay but from an inherent sense of simplicity, straight lines, and a mental discipline that prevents any form of excess.

In the Mehrauli area, not far from Qutub Minar, gifts shops, jewellery stores, designer boutiques and outlets for expensive imported accessories have been proliferating in recent years

I have attended, in this area, and in other places of the city, several inaugural ceremonies, of showrooms of "big" brands, such as Vuitton, Cartier, or Ralph Lauren. These inaugurations are relatively frequent today among many of the "new rich" of New Delhi society. It makes the initial phase, towards the end of the 1900s and at the beginning of the 2000s, seem quite distant when such renowned products appeared in India for the first time, and were not destined solely for the royalty.

Most of the conversations that take place at such inaugurations revolve around an endless list of restaurants and hotels, in an incessant whirl of names of places where such or such person has just been, or will be going soon. There is usually no possible space in these brief exchanges, with few exceptions of course, for serious topics or content. It is true that this is a universal phenomenon, this trivialization of conversation, of words. Nothing means what it means or used to. Words like historical, mythical, mystical, philosophy and alchemy were used in very special contexts and with prior explanation. Today they are used indiscriminately for advertisements and any triviality.

From the days of the "hyperguru" Bhagwan Rajneesh, later known as Osho, there is a tendency on the part of the new age spiritualists not to despise wealth, even ostentatious wealth, but rather quite the opposite. They start from the premise that such abundance is not contrary to meditation and yogic practices, which is partly true, but then make a qualitative leap to go beyond and postulate that only the one who is free from the daily concerns of subsistence is in a relaxed and conducive situation to perform spiritually. These new gurus repeat ad nauseum that a harmony between both extremes must be sought—the excessive desire for possession and total detachment. The summary of such an incessant search is always this—harmony, proportion, counterweight, symmetry, and other synonyms that try to make their own sense, of this attractive though dangerous combination. One ought to object that the problem lies in the fact that few take its application seriously, to actually put it into practice, which is why it remains a mere theory, and usually the material end ends up winning.

Actually, the ultimate problem of wealth in relation to spirituality is not possession of many or few things, which is always relative to the situation of each one, but that such things do not possess us. It is painful when one sees people, especially those who have become enriched quickly, as unprotected, naked, personally unarmed against their properties. In other words, these beings with the keys of multiple properties in their pockets, seem like children of what they own and not their lords. It is pathetic, in fact, to see them unable to go even a step beyond where they are, because they are tied to their possessions, and are forced incessantly to do what these objects force them to do.

At present, one of the great dangers for the country is that the vast majority of the middle class, not having had the ability to possess anything for a long time, now suffers from a bulimia of brands and objects…an avalanche of things that are often useless. This incipient phenomenon may be inevitable, though in reality only a small percentage of the population have access to the big local and foreign brands that have taken over India. This is undoubtedly something dangerous, because until yesterday such an obvious imbalance of opportunities was not even seen, while today it is made evident by television and the media, which can create inevitable envies.

One afternoon, I think sometime mid-March, before the heat had set in, I was invited to a classic car show and contest called Concours d'élégance, organized by a well-known brand of Swiss watches. The meeting and exhibition took place at the Jaipur Grounds, as it was known in British times since it apparently housed one of the racing tracks, near the current office and residence of the Prime Minister. Seeing them there all together, those admirable exemplars of whimsical shapes and colours, each and every one of them unique in its particular design, they looked exactly what they were—glories of a world already far away! Glories of a vanished world! In contrast, the cars that today's new rich seek do not display beauty, or show elegance that comes with unique design, aesthetic contours, and advanced mechanics. What interests them is a show of aggression, and a shallow display of economic resources. The majority of those magnificent cars seen there that afternoon, almost eighty of them, had once belonged to some of the five hundred princes, referred to as Maharajas, and Nawabs, among other titles in pre-independence India.

Since 1892, when Maharaja Rajinder Singh of Patiala purchased and brought the first car to India, a De Dion-Bouton, until the late forties of the last century, many more jewels on four wheels, of clockwork precision were imported, via a long journey from the Old Continent. I imagined these beautiful motors, new and bright under tarpaulins in the holds of ships. I evoked them in my imagination traversing the Mediterranean, through the Suez Canal, and after curving round the Arabian Gulf, heading towards the waters of the Indian Ocean. One third of all brands that were imported to India, in that golden period were Rolls Royces. This legendary Derby firm, crowned by the Spirit of Ecstasy insignia, has conferred its hallmark on most exquisitely designed and exclusive cars. India was not an exception to this trend of the richest to own such a brand. In fact, it was the paradise par excellence for these machines that "never break down". The best known of them all still exists, known as "The Star of India", an orange and aluminium Rolls Royce Phantom I of 1926.

I was specially interested in the cars from before the Second World War, and but for some beautiful exceptions, I didn't find the American cars too fetching. Huge, yes, but in general coarse, with muscular forms, and quite obviously out of an assembly line, representative of a country that in the years before and after the war, began to push its way around throughout the world. Absolutely contrary to them are the European jewels, especially British, but also Italian and German, unique pieces from the moment they left the factory, and worthy of specific and exclusive names for each of them.

There in the front line could be seen a Blue Rolls, a Phantom II Drophead Coupe, registered in Jodhpur N-1, belonging to Maharaj Gaj Singhji of Jodhpur. A little further a Packard 740, 1937 model belonging to the Maharaja of Jaipur, a Buy de Soto of 1929, a Delage D8 120s. Beautiful roadster, as also a Morgan Plus 4 of 1951, a Jaguar XK120 of 1951, a Triumph TR 3 of 1955. Beyond them, an impressive Hispano-Swiss K6 Cabriolet of 1934, belonging to Yuvraj Vishwaraj Singh of Udaipur.

Seen from the viewing gallery, these ancient and majestic automobiles sparkled in the esplanade below as if they were gems.

Yes, for anyone who values them, it's not an exaggeration to call them that because all those pieces glittered like precious stones—the green ones like emeralds, the blue like sapphires, the red like rubies. Yes, it was a veritable open-air—jewellery mart! These were obviously not vehicles to just move around in, to be used to go to the workplace. They were very special specimens, meant for unique occasions, but now asleep in a long slumber as the crowning moment of their privileged and complex lives was over. They rest their aching iron bones in air-conditioned garages of huge mansions, and are seen only on rare occasions, sporadically erupting in the nondescript automotive landscape, striking one with flashes of their forgotten beauty.

It was a pleasure to behold that scene, otherwise familiar to me from other occasions in different venues. It was a delight to watch all the proud owners or collaborators near their jewels, open to anyone who wanted to ask them about how they had preserved them, protected them from the ravages of time, or restored them thoroughly after they had fallen in some cases, into the most complete ruin. In between one of the rides in the cars, I was introduced by a friend to one of the Indian guests, who in turn introduced me to the honorary president of the panel that was to judge those enviable pieces from another era. The Duke of Kent, cousin of the Queen of England, had been invited. When I told him that I was a Spanish architect who had been living in New Delhi for a while, he congratulated me, and told me that his granddaughter had studied my mother tongue, and that he himself would like to learn it, but that he was already perhaps "a bit too old".

Not far away from us was the turquoise blue Bentley of none other than Gayatri Devi, the glamorous Maharani of Jaipur who had stunned the world and the India of her times. A little beyond was parked a Rolls Royce 25 HP of 1932, of the Maharaja of Mandi, next to them a beautiful Hispano-Suiza K6 Cabriolet of 1935, and a sky blue Bentley Mr VI of 1949 of the Maharaja of Mysore. Then there were also other makes of the time, now totally unknown, such as Minerva, Steyr, Moon, or Wolseley.

Currently many of them belong to the new rich, who display them in their mansions as trophies, or they are used for weddings by rental agencies. All of them true treasures on four wheels, their noble carriages with steering wheel and brakes handcrafted pieces with chiselled crystals, and unique details. Nothing more farther, it would seem, from today's cars, with their tin plate sheets and plastic! All of them alike, copied in a most shameless way, as if applying "singular thinking" to cars, giving them a very similar appearance, whether small or large, expensive or cheap—so that all end up looking exactly like each other!

Today, we know with some precision that some 60 million years ago what we identify as India began a long journey north, as if it had been a great ship of rocks and sand, formed by the vagaries of the Earth far from where we walk on it today. At the southern end of the planet, almost in Antarctica, in those remote times it was linked to Africa and Australia, as is a known fact. It was in that area where a slow breakdown began that would take an eternity in human terms, but conceived in terms of the period of formation of the planet, it was a simple journey of rearrangement. Up there, in the end, as though fulfilling a mission decreed by someone or something, it arrived at its present location with that typically triangular figure that we identify on the map obviously and unmistakably as India. Our India!

The Earth's crust is formed by a layer of large rocky fragments which are articulated with each other in the form of shapeless and heterogeneous vertebrae, pressed by inconceivable forces that exert mute displacements, hardly visible between them. The colossal compression thrusts that arose from the collision between the tectonic plates, from the extreme south and the Eurasian plate, caused an unusual mountain elevation, the highest on Earth, giving the Himalayas a typically alpine orogeny. And this kind of force continues to push the mountain range up—about three centimetres every hundred years! If there had been then a witness to such geological epics, it could have been said that a very precise project was drawn in that continental drift. It was as if the birth of Tibet was already planned as a direct consequence of such a collision. In fact, it was as if it was foreseen that a people as unique as the Tibetans, with their enigmatic rites and ancient religions, would settle on the eternal snows and the high mountains that emerged from the encounter of Eurasia with that great island adrift that we call Indias. It seems that this equally singular nation, which from a remote past, has gone through the ages in one piece, was "in a hurry" to arrive at the place it occupies today in the South of the Asian Continent. Here it is at last! It is bounded by the great mountain range to the North, and its Indian and Arabian oceans on both sides, forming borders that are as natural as they are recognizable.

Thanks to the recent geological studies from the Universities of Sydney and Southern California, that it has been possible, by means of satellite detection, to determine quite accurately, when the first continental encounter with this piece of land took place, which we today associate with yoga, curry and Bollywood. Indeed, it was long known that the Himalayas were the consequence of a colossal collision in the Indian Ocean, millions of years after the tectonic plate formed by Antarctica and present-day Africa and Australia, which made up an old supercontinent known as Gondwana. This continent in turn came from Pangea, the only continent that the

Earth had after its formation. After the Earth was covered by the seas, it broke about 200 million years ago, and got divided into the block of the Northern Hemisphere, called Eurasia, and the rest. What has been possible to specify, according to these latest studies, are such apparently inconceivable details, such as how fast India travelled to the North in that almost eternal and lonely, although determined journey: about 15 centimetres on average a year! Less than the palm of a hand!

India is not an island! Just look at the map! The Eastern and Western coasts, however, together with the clear barrier of the North, forced its flora and fauna to reconstitute this vast territory from time immemorial into a space that suggests insularity. This reality gives it certain island characteristics, such as its inhabitants being mentally far from their own neighbours. It has, actually, quite a few phenomena reminiscent of the islands, such as the numerous endemic species of plants and animals. As is known, in the long period of adaptation, over thousands, or millions of years, the species that came to the islands to survive consolidated their "ecological niches". Some such species are very primitive, native to India, with ancestors that had journeyed adrift on to this land for an inconceivable time, while others hail from neighbouring territories. This was, in effect, a long process until both ecosystems, the insular and the continental, stabilized in a common environment. At about four and a half million square kilometres, the Indian subcontinent, or as it was known before the 1947 Partition, with more than 1.5 billion people, a quarter of the world's population, and one of the highest densities of people per square kilometre (more than 350), it includes India, Pakistan, Bangladesh, and Nepal. Another possible historical name would be Hindustan, "the country of the Indians", although this would only refer to India, something that its neighbours would not like very much, and South Asia, another possibility, which as a vaguer and more neutral term, would include several other countries like Afghanistan or Burma.

Many countries, groups, or individuals consider themselves absolutely unique, in a somewhat forced, and even narcissistic manner, perhaps for fear of insignificance, oblivion, or simply disappearing, as is unfortunately happening today with nationalisms of big or small variety, in various parts of the world. In India, in fact, it happens in reverse, at least as far as the country is concerned. The vast majority of its inhabitants are not seen as especially unique, although they are! Few of the old nations treasure such an enormous number of languages, cultures, religions, races and ethnic groups on Earth. And yet, compared to the rest of the world, India displays a clear unity which is well-differentiated. The consequence, however, of this multiple reality in India, involves a constant challenge of maintaining such diversity of identities, without impoverishing or simplifying their variety. All India Radio, for example, broadcasts in 24 languages and 146 dialects, since there are 24 official languages here, written in 13 different scripts, and more than 700 dialects. In addition to Hindi and English, these are the other 22 official languages: Assamese and Bodo (Assam), Bengali (Tripura and West Bengal), Kashmiri and Dogri (Jammu and Kashmir), Gujarati (Gujarat), Kannada (Karnataka), Konkani (Goa), Maithili (Bihar), Malayalam (Kerala), Manipuri or Meitei (Manipur), Marathi (Maharashtra), Nepali (Sikkim), Oriya (Orissa), Panjabi (Punjab), Portuguese (Goa and various places), Sanskrit (sacred language), Santhali (Jharkhand, Assam, etc.), Sindhi (former Sind province), Tamil (Tamil Nadu), Telugu (Andhra Pradesh), Urdu (Jammu and Kashmir). And despite having so many languages, India does not have a national language!

Since Nehru's speech to the nation on 15 August 1947, after Independence, in which he spoke of India as an achievement of "unity in diversity", this slogan has served as the engine for its unification and preservation. "Some kind of unity has occupied the mind of India since the dawn of civilization. That unity was not conceived as something imposed from outside, a standardization of externals or even of beliefs. It was something deeper and within its fold, the widest tolerance of belief and customs was practiced and every variety acknowledged and even encouraged", wrote Jawaharlal Nehru in *The Discovery of India*.

Something is indeed unique in this singular country! If this were not the case, travellers who decide to visit India, and do so with genuine interest, would not emphasize that on their return they "see the world differently". If there is anything that such western travellers agree on, both those of past times and the present day it is that after visiting India there is an unequivocal transformation that is difficult to define. It is spontaneous! It just happens! The most varied people will declare that their own existence, or rather, their way of looking at it, is no longer the same as it was before the trip. The priorities, the values, are the ones that mutate to a higher level. All those who visit India emphasize that even in the midst of the most absolute misery smiles arise. Especially in children and women. They also underline that people are generally friendly no matter how poor they are, something that does not happen in African or Latin American lands, where violence and robberies are common. In India it happens but only marginally. It is true that India is a culture full of artistic and spiritual riches, and equally full of deficiencies in personal means of existence, which simultaneously or consecutively arouse disgust or admiration among those who pass through it.

The streets and roads of India are often a second jungle with the unceasing roar of horns, clang and rattle of trains, revving of motorcycles and noxious fumes. Although the globetrotter certainly does not find them as horrifying here as in other places, and sometimes, only sometimes, it is the chaos, linked to temples and other elements, that reveals itself as paradoxical beauty, difficult to explain or analyze. Depending on luck, one may have a good or bad trip. What is unequivocal, however, is the residue from the experience. A constant is that no one declares oneself neutral after their passage through India. You either reject or love! With all the necessary nuances in the latter case, and none in the former. In this regard, the words of the great American writer, Mark Twain, who in 1896 enjoyed a long journey through this admired Asian country, are famous. "So far as I am able to judge, nothing has been left undone, either by man or nature, to make India the most extraordinary country that the sun visits on his rounds. Nothing seems to have been forgotten, nothing overlooked." Twain, a lover of the Mississippi River, refers to a unique nation in terms of the number of its capital contributions to humanity, from the world of spirituality to that of art, mythology and music, literature, and science as well.

"India is intense!" "It is a country of extremes in the good and the bad!" Such are the phrases that one hears most, and are shared most among travellers of fairly different persuasions. Indeed, if there is something that India cannot really be accused of, whether in the large figures or in private experiences, it is being "light", being perceived light or easily digestible. Everything in her carries its time of gestation, its process of maturity, necessarily slow, and this period is not something one controls. It is always Mother India who decides! Half measures don't work here! India can, and must, be experienced, as indeed it is, intensely, whether you like it or not, every minute you stay here. For some reason, its manifestations can never be reasoned, or its influence explained. In any case, precious little is achieved by doing so. The manner in which Western logic is postulated, she tells you, is impossible for it to work. But the reality, even though it is chaos in motion personified, is there, with its growth of 7.3 per cent per year of GDP! Without ceasing to be chaos in motion!

There is no linear continuity here, something foreseen and predictable, in the sense in which Europeans are used to, which in the language of aviation is called "auto-pilot." As is known, this term is used in air navigation when the commander of an aircraft has stabilized it after ascending, going beyond the clouds and most such atmospheric phenomena that could interfere with the flight, when the mentioned pilot mode is activated. Perhaps there is no other country which would be more contrary to any likelihood of "autopilot"! Nothing can ever be taken for granted or as certain here, even though the circumstances may seem lasting and predictable at first sight… The reason is that the next moment, perhaps everything will be interrupted, or the thread of what we are doing will simply disappear. What is certain is that ruptures happen much more frequently than continuity! Sudden stops bring us back to the point zero of what we were dealing with, and we have to start our task from the beginning!

Whether you go to one or the other of its cardinal points, from north to south, from east to west, there is something intangible, something common that floats throughout India, which beyond its infinite variety, makes this country identifiable as what it is, and not something else. However, there are many different Indias! One's appreciation changes according to the circuit, the medium where one enters. Everything has the potential to quickly and inadvertently turn into its opposite—the beautiful in horrendous, the sweet in bitter, the thick in fine, the pompous in miserable, or perhaps the other way around. What seems easiest in appearance, such as a short commute, a daily chore, or the smallest bureaucratic process, can suddenly become a nightmare.

There is an enormous range of possibilities in the country, of experiences close to the world of spirituality, aesthetic pleasure and the journey of unending discoveries, as perhaps cannot be had elsewhere in the world. However, it takes a lot of energy and time to get close to such places, such experiences, because they are not easily accessible. Those endless sunsets, of an impossible red, that seem to levitate the sands and the water on the beach of Panjim, for example. Travelling the highest road in the world in Ladakh, with euphoria as well as with paucity of oxygen, breathing to the limit. Travelling along the Narmada River, perhaps the cleanest in India, from the point where it is born and further on, in the middle of your way, in Mandu, to see some inconceivable palaces, discovered after climbing a mountain in the middle of nowhere. It is all quite incomparable! But also difficult to get to!

From the southern tip of the Indian subcontinent, in Kanyakumari, to the Himalayas in the North, from the Arabian Sea in the West, to the Bay of Bengal in the direction of sunrise, 363 distinct communities are mentioned by name in the Mahabharata. Such is the variety of these people, not only in the past, but in the present, that the Indian Government undertook, between 1984 and 1996, a great task that had not been done until then. It was the The People of India Project, which managed to identify by name almost five thousand communities (4,694) with their own defined identity, of which 2,205 are the main. In addition, 324 languages and core dialects were registered, of which 25 have their own script. In this great diversity, the common racial and cultural genes far outnumber those that are different and divergent. It should be noted that although all communities identify with one or several religions, none do so with a single ethnicity or ethnic group, although they do identify with certain group of languages.

Although today India appears to us as a fairly identifiable, closed and homogeneous cluster, despite its diversity of languages, races and creeds, it is what one calls a unifying culture that was able to absorb numerous foreign elements, especially from the Mesopotamian, Persian, and Greek world in Antiquity, as well as Arabic and Iranian in the Middle Ages, and more recently from the Western world, be it British, European, or American. The key to its continuity as a nation has been the fabulous integration of such different, and even contrary elements that it has exercised with intense syncretism, and its own unmistakable touch. From the most seasoned and hard ingredients, originating from the arid Afghan lands, to the sweetest and softest ones, such as those from the southern coasts, the most heterogeneous elements exist together, they draw strong contrasts for us, like a rock against a palm tree, the harsh and severe taste of the desert as against the bituminous and sweet flavours of the mangroves.

India is a great nurturing mother! It is as instinctive as it is contradictory! It snatches life as inexplicably as it gives! There is no doubt that even today deep and indelible roots coexist in everything that shapes the country. And religion is a living example of this! There is no one God, but several millions, whom we identify as divinities, avatars of the three main deities. Such is the well-known Trimurti, with Vishnu, the Preserver of the cosmos, Shiva, its Destroyer, and Brahma, its theoretical Creator. However, even Brahma, the Supreme Being appears most of the times in old writings and traditions as an unnamed reality, about whom it cannot even be affirmed that it possesses or lacks a name, since to do so would be to presuppose its uncertain existence. This is a terrain in which a mystery and a symbol are only a prelude to other symbols and other deeper hidden mysteries. Words like death, energy or nature are very different here from what they mean or imply in the West, with differences not of nuance, but of basic concept. Since ancient times, this land has accumulated all the imaginable adventures not only of the spirit, but also of the body, from the outer skin, to the very core, both in relation to the earth and to the cosmos. This is an immense accumulated heritage that is no longer solely Indian, but of all humanity.

In what concerns its social and economic structure, its daily operation, however, it is as if it were an old and immense engine that was squeaking and creaking because it was functioning out of rhythm at every step. India is a country with infinite gears and long drive belts that bring together very diverse and distant parts, both in time and space. Some are dazzling, fascinating, while others are decayed and rusty, all loudly calling for a more fluid and viable functioning, fairer to its distant castes and brutally contrasted social levels. Such rusty and obsolete gears endeavour hard to shake hands with others from the 21st century. But replacing the exhausted is postponed time and again, perhaps due to apathy, or more likely due to a reluctance to make real investments in the future. A future in which there is perhaps not much credence!

The attempt to respect the essence of its culture, despite the suffering, corruption, the blatantly aggressive capitalism concentrated in very few hands and the endless dysfunctions, is not just fascinating, it is compelling.

Indians are not competitive in many sectors, in terms of production management and quality compared to the large industrialized countries, but they are at a precise point, reached with some effort, and they know that they must be counted. India's "future" is spoken about most firmly, but it is often difficult to demonstrate it in its own terrain. The problem is that when that "future" will arrive is uncertain, and when it does it is definitively going to leave two thirds of the country's population in the lurch. It's been "emerging" for a long time! But that emerging costs a lot!

Of the approximately 1.3 billion people who inhabit India, almost 70 per cent live in rural areas, and an increasing 30 per cent in urban centres. Half of its population is under 25 years old, making it one of the youngest countries, with about 75,000 births a day, which is equivalent to about fifty new souls every minute, and almost one a second. Dizzying, compared to Spain! Or a good part of Europe, which at most aspires to balance the number of deceased with few births.

Such an overpopulation makes possible unique phenomena on the planet, such as the massive gathering of yogis, sadhus, saints and all kinds of imaginable people, at what is known as the Kumbha Mela, which is celebrated in certain sacred places in the country. One of the most extraordinary in recent times was the one held in Allahabad in 2013, where approximately one hundred million people could be seen as a great moving mass by the satellites orbiting the Earth!!! These peak moments of mass gathering occur, when according to Vedic astrology (*jyotish*), Jupiter enters the constellation Aquarius (*kumbha*) every three years, and once every 12 years resulting in the great Kumbha Mela. The origin of this festival, in which renunciates and ascetics of all kinds demonstrate that they do not suffer from any agoraphobia, lies in the rites of propitiation for good harvests, which are performed at the sowing season. In these rites, the water of the rivers, and especially that of the sacred Ganges, harbours the symbolic as well as the material meaning of making the grain germinate on the earth, of opening the shadows of the depths to light. The celebration of such an ancient ceremony may have begun in the Mohenjo-Daro civilization, and is linked to fertility rites that, with a more or less explicit sexuality, take place throughout the country.

Equally unthinkable anywhere else on the planet, and related to the very high population, given that a state like Uttar Pradesh has more inhabitants than all of Japan, rare events occur, such as the planting of almost 67 million trees in half a day in the state of Madhya Pradesh in 2017, earning it a place in the Guinness Book of Records! I mean, in 12 hours! An event in which more than a million volunteers took part. Such a feat was far from unique. Other similar events, though with somewhat lower figures, had taken place in earlier years in various states such as Maharashtra, Kerala and Uttar Pradesh. Which other country is capable of mobilizing a million people, for an altruistic end like this? The satellite photographs also testify that while in recent decades there has been great deforestation around the world, in India, as always against the current with the rest, this time in a good way, there has been an increase in the green cover. All this in the midst of an amazing biodiversity, with more than one hundred national parks, and more than five hundred natural sanctuaries.

India represents a kind of great laboratory, with extreme and contrasting elements in every field—social, religious, economic, and cultural. Floods and droughts, the two big challenges for much of the Earth, symbolize in India extremes of excess and deficiency, which it must constantly face. The gap between the one and the other experience is such an obvious reality, that perhaps there is little reflection on this particularity by the Indians themselves. In few places on the planet are the most beautiful surroundings or monuments assaulted by dirt or afflicted by utter neglect and the sublime inhabits the terrifying. In terms of GDP, geographic size and growing regional influence, India is a superpower; however, in other aspects, such as natural disasters and accidents, as also territorial conflicts and abject poverty, it is visibly part of what is known as the Third World. Despite this, it is a nation increasingly perceived throughout the world as a "bridge" between East and West, as a rich and essential resource for all humanity, not yet very explicit in its development, but with an undoubted force of cohesion, of integration of many contradictory and apparently incompatible components! India today has an important role to play in multiple fields and serve as a model for other cultures in maintaining the balance between the material and the spiritual. And a new paradox! It undoubtedly has the ingredients to become such a model and reach that role at some point, but has not been able to become one for itself, yet.

The obvious gaps between India and the West are not so much scientific, or technological, but social, with regard to labour conditions, a dignified life for an extensive middle class, simplification of bureaucratic red tape, in short, a better "quality of life", hitherto unknown to most of its population. That today is summarized in maximizing the most basic sectors—Employment, Education, Housing, Health, Transport, and Food.

After a few decades of some stability on the international scene, except for the collapse of the Soviet world, many of the countries, especially in Asia, are readjusting to a new economic, political, and specially a new social situation. Among them is the enclave of Hong Kong, Singapore, Korea, and Indonesia. These circumstances are the result of new economic equations in the world and the growing incidence of increasingly hybrid societies, as well as the omnipresence of China in all fields, the supply of cheap labour being just one of them. India is by no means an exception to this new changed scenario. It is rather one of the main protagonists. As Europe's preferred partner, India should be privileged in Asia over China. Starting with the Asian campaign of Alexander the Great, there are numerous cultural connections since antiquity which facilitate mutual understanding between the Indo-European, Eastern and Western spheres. There is the added aspect of India not being in competition with Europe, unlike China; rather, there is a potential common interest in the exchange of raw and industrial materials, technology, software, etc.

And yet, despite the many steps towards mutual approximation in recent times, India still looks at Europe with some suspicion, perhaps due to the colonialist aftertaste, linked to its experience with Great Britain, and perhaps, due to its lack of interaction with the rest of the "Old Continent". India knows it in general, as superficially as European tourists know India! Information about India is usually reduced to a few proper names, to various stereotypes such as yoga and Ayurveda. Indian citizens, on their part, traditionally seek to reside or to spend their vacations only in Anglophone cities/countries and Anglo-Saxon habits, such as the USA, Canada, or Australia. Without a doubt, Latin Europe (Spain, Portugal, Italy, and France), and Latin America, with which they have common traits of character, rather than culture and religion, would be a useful and pleasant discovery, as it has already been for many artists, intellectuals, and diplomats. Much remains to be investigated mutually, by both parties. It should be done by the Indians who until now have remained from the non-English-speaking world by choice.

There is a perception among the Indians that Europe is excessively protectionist, which is true to a certain extent. But then it should be remembered that India is protectionism in its purest form! There is a mirror effect! Most Indians see Europe as a nosy, questioning continent, that likes to give advice it would do well to apply to itself.

In this difficult beginning of the 21st century, with new ways of communications and possibilities through internet, the most advanced models of work and society, it is evident that a world, relatively stable up to now, is dying, while a new hybrid paradigm that concerns every human sphere is about to emerge, if it hasn't already happened! At the same time, there is a massive relocation of companies in the world, and a brutal competition among numerous countries, especially from China and the USA. At the same time, several multinational companies and banking groups transcend all these countries. While the great material explosion is notorious, a spiritual one is also happening, though much smaller and subterranean, but equally intense. Everything has accelerated inconceivably in recent years in every imaginable direction! The future lacks the defined centres as have existed up to now!

Another point that introduces a certain distortion in the possible and desirable smooth relationship between India and Europe is that many enlightened Indians think that in reality there is no common European culture, rather there are fragments, and they are as many as there are countries! This is partly true, if we look at the concrete data of each country on social spending, production, etc., but it is true only in case of the economy and foreign relations, where there are individual commercial and national interests involved. Despite such differences, in many other areas such as thought and art, it is clear, however, that there were many historical movements, like the Gothic and the Renaissance, that reveal very close and complementary identities within Europe. Now, it is clear that due to the aforementioned misgivings and lack of knowledge, Indian leaders prefer the established great powers, such as China, the United States, Japan, and the emerging Asian countries who are its privileged neighbours, over Europe, except for specific, well-defined interests, like German technology. Regarding global governance, decision-makers in New Delhi may harbour fears that it will be Europe's long-industrialized economies that will lead the way, and push only the countries in which they are interested, while the emerging economies will be relegated to the limited circle of merely buyers. In the field of ideas, however, it could be said that there is an undoubted, although limited, discretionary admiration for Europe in India vis-a-vis its economic protectionism. In fields such as the division of powers enshrined by Montesquieu's theory, the rule of law, and the parliamentary system, along with everything that accompanies these interrelated concepts, namely the rights and initiatives of civil society, which amounts to greater freedom, European political influences of a general nature can be detected in the idea of Indian nationalism itself. And the very specific influence exerted by Tolstoy on Gandhi.

As a former ambassador to India recently commented, "Asians want the welfare and democracy of the European Union—nobody wants to live like the Chinese or the United Arab Emirates, even if they are very rich", adding that although China grows somewhat more (10 per cent) than India (9 per cent), democracy makes the latter more stable, something that represents a definite advantage for India even in the medium term. In sum, India's relationship with the West is fundamentally ambiguous, since it is in the throes of a transition, a period which goes from post-colonial India, to a higher status as a sovereign country with a presence in the international scene, and in which it seeks a new role in this multipolar world.

India is rich in interpretations of how everything in the cosmos arose. According to an old Indian legend, Lord Brahma, the creator, felt immensely lonely before there was anything in the universe, during what is known as the Night of Brahma. According to this mythological story, to get out of his languor and boredom, the great Being decided to create a beautiful goddess with whom to have fun in a great game (*lila*). She was named Maya, and shortly before beginning her existence she imposed a condition on the Maker. She demanded that he bring forth the cosmos with all its galaxies, stars, and planets, plus life and animals. Not content with just that, she asked Brahma that beyond the inert elements, the celestial bodies and living beings, he create conscious beings, who would be capable of admiring his great Work, the Cosmos. When this was done, with the coming into existence of the human being, and her wish fulfilled, Brahma asked Maya when they were going to start the *lila*, at which she immediately cut him into infinite pieces, carefully placing each one inside of every human being. "This is the moment", she said, "when the game really begins." And this consisted not only of a loving frolic, but also of something that according to legend, Brahma did not suspect—that he, the Creator God, had to forget who he was, having to search for himself in each and every existing being. Maya had invented the dream of the highest consciousness, and from that moment Brahma tries to remember who he is, unaware of his own identity, confined as he is within men. Beyond dream, and the robes of existence, that which inhabits the human being, that which can awaken, and remember its true divine nature, is pure consciousness, the spirit, the divine spark. That which does not sleep! That which is always awake!

Brahma, curiously, was hardly ever worshipped in India, and the fact that there are only two temples (the most famous in Pushkar) dedicated to him proves this.The other two Trimurti divinities, Shiva and Vishnu, have countless sanctuaries throughout the country.

The moral of this amazing fable is that when humans wake up from their dream of existence, and stop believing that they are just a piece of matter, they will become Brahma again. According to current astrophysics, the duration of such a divine "blink" between Night and Day is about 13.7 billion human years. The dream of this great Being is equivalent to an immeasurable universal cycle that has been represented in various legends as a kind of "blink". Every time he closes his eyes, the universe contracts until it disappears, and when he opens them again, the cosmos comes into existence, expanding once again.

This image of a supreme God who breathes life and existence into the universe with alternate and infinite, inconceivably long cycles of day and night, always seemed to me very imaginative, and suggestive of great plausibility for that huge mystery of the cosmos, linked to our origin as beings who have become aware of it all. In addition, it has unexpected echoes in current astronomy, with the hypothesis of successive big bang and big crash creations and implosions with a never-ending beginning and end. It is a chain of infinite links in which each and every one becomes invisible before giving birth to the next. The beat of a heart, enormously large as well as small, opening and closing like a flower with each new day, with a programmed intermittence, with an ultimate meaning ignored even by the gods themselves.

Vedanta establishes that the supreme, non-personalized God (Brahman), is the only reality of the universe. Everything else does not have a life of its own, but one that is offered, and only constitutes an illusion (maya) in the way it manifests itself. Vedanta also postulates that the duality that we constantly perceive in the world between pleasure and pain, between light and shadow, is due to the ignorance of the very nature of reality, which is not dual in itself, but only presents ranges, of differences in degree. This forces us to revise the usual relationship of distance and differentiation between the conscious subject, us, and the objects of perception, since both are more intertwined than they appear on the surface. They are not the same, they do not lose their individual location and at the same time they are not different. This, though paradoxical, is the deepest insight one can have about the experience of reality! It means that the separation, the distinction between subject and object on which our classical theory of knowledge is based, does not exist in the way we consider it, rather both instances are appearances, very small facets of an all-encompassing network of a non-dual Consciousness. There are no two separate worlds here, as there are in Platonism: the Ideal one and that of the shadows, rather a single reality, with diverse manifestations.

Linked to the conclusions and teachings of the Vedas, the best-known way of Vedanta is the *Advaita* ("not two" in Sanskrit), and its first theorist is the famous philosopher Shankara (788–820), who claims that the ultimate message of the Upanishads is Unity. This is the culmination of wisdom in Hinduism, known as *Sanatana Dharma*, or Eternal Religion, beyond names and sects. It means that all things are interconnected, even if they simultaneously maintain their uniqueness. This non-dualistic vision defends the essential unity between the soul (atman) and the ultimate divinity (Brahman). Unity of origin and manifestation. It supposes the union of a total being coexisting with the rest of the beings and elements, as expressed by the metaphor of the "network of Indra", or of the "Pearls of Indra".

The image of dewdrops on a spider's web beautifully stages two basic concepts of Mahayana Buddhism, which are emptiness and reciprocal dependence on everything that exists. The idea is taken from the Hindu Cosmology (Puranas), in which the Pearls of Indra are an infinite network of threads, or cords, that like a hologram, occupy, and unite the entire universe. According to the very recent "string theory", just like those of a musical instrument, such strings would vibrate in different dimensions and in different ways, uniting everything that exists, from the micro to the macrocosm.

In Indian mythology, Shiva, the singular divinity who knows how to recharge himself with the elements, water and fire, is characterized by the most difficult and extreme attitudes, and risky heroism. Unlike other divinities, nobody knows his origin or his possible ancestors, precursors or antecedents!

Among his many attributes, Shiva is Nilakantha, one who has a blue throat since he drank poison. Even among the gods he is distinguished by being the only one who ingests poison! He is unique in overcoming any possible risk of death, devastation, and disappearance. According to the legend, he sensed the onset of pain from the lethal drink, but he did not let the drink get into him, it does not reach his inside. The potion stays in the throat, and never manages to penetrate the heart (*hridaya*)!

The fact that all this takes place in the throat, where as per yoga, the *buddhi* resides, the mind that judges and decides, that discriminates, and ultimately filters off the poison is significant. That dark drink symbolizes ordinary emotions, the lethal residue of existence and the ego. It is what must be transformed, so that life and consciousness reach their maximum expression and final freedom in this dense universe. It's like opening the window, and turning darkness into light by the force of one's will! Beyond mundane experiences and ordinary life, basic emotions and feelings (bhavas), there are essences (rasas), which act as a perfume exhaled by the flower of our experience, traditionally classified into the basis of Indian art—disgust, love, anger, joy, courage, fear, compassion, wonder and peace. At their lowest and densest level, rasas are poisonous, highly toxic, driven only by fear and hatred. However, empowered by the elements, the most graceful and sublime rasas lead souls to higher states of consciousness, in which there is love and identification. Real and lasting peace is only reached after crossing the most varied dangers and putting oneself to the test, until tasting that everlasting nectar, the internal soma, which is unending.

For this, however, it is necessary to transcend the ego. One must act only with the highest essences (rasas), those that approach pure consciousness, and abandon the others. Otherwise, one is captured, taken prisoner by the mundane and banal world.

Shiva is also the one who knows how to extract the elixir, the Soma, from any circumstance. He is the one who knows how to get the best and brightest from no matter what situation or object, however difficult they may be, operating through all of them like a seasoned acrobat. This unusual Being seems to tell us that everything in life can equally act as poison or ambrosia, depending on how it is faced and who does it. Everything is mind! Everything is consciousness! It therefore depends on the way in which the poison is swallowed and transformed, on how it is made, and how finally the body assimilates it. It is the state of quietude, of inner peace that dominates the Lord of the Yogis, the axis of the universe, which is what makes this magical transformation possible.

Shiva's great work is *mahapralaya*, creative destruction, the cyclical dissolution of all that is created, in order to be able to remake it again. His role is doubly difficult, because it means the destruction of the cosmos, seeking the emergence of what is purest and most enduring. That is why in many of his representations, he wears a garland of human heads, cut off with his trident *trishul*, as a symbol of the sacrifice necessary for renewal of life. This does not mean in any way that he is an evil being or anything close to that, it rather refers to the need for renewal inherent in Nature.

Shiva is also the great lord of time. He dominates it, he is beyond the dimensions of space and time and is unaffected by them. He never loses pace or rhythm! He has the secret of the momentary and of eternity, of becoming the axis of everything that happens, thus being both static and dynamic, something that is especially appreciated in his representation as Nataraja, the king of cosmic dance.

In this graceful and beautiful form, Shiva Nataraja, dances in the centre of an igneous circle (*prabha mandala*), which in Indian mythology symbolizes the same fire that gave rise to and keeps the cosmos alive. It is located in its very centre, at the point known as Chidambaram. Mahadeva, the great god, stands with his right leg slightly bent and his left leg raised upwards across his body, suggesting an ecstatic dance in which all the virtues are imprinted. He is graceful, energetic and subtle all at the same time!

This famous representation of him as the four-armed god, symbolizes his performance in the earthly and heavenly world. Both double arms also refer to the two faces or phases of everything that exists, of creation (*ananda tandava*), and of destruction (*rudra tandava*). In his upper right hand, he holds the *damaru*, an instrument that symbolizes the time and rhythm of Creation. It reveals to the human being the veils of maya, of the illusory, and helps him to find the centre of his heart, which is the place where the higher realities are located. His lower right hand touches his matted locks which symbolizes the Ganges river with its renewal, as a point of contact between heaven and earth. In his upper left hand, he holds the fire of life, with its ability to create and destroy. Beneath him, with his right leg slightly arched, he steps on the dwarf, or demon Apasmara, signifying victory over evil and ignorance.

The figure of Nataraja attracts attention for the serenity of his face, with his eyes half closed and concentrated on his inner peace. He is absent, and at the same time he is an absolute present. Sometimes, in the bronze statues in which he is represented (the most beautiful are those of Tamil Nadu, cast in seven metals), he is shown with a smile which is reminiscent of that of the Buddha, with subtle suggestions of calm and transcendence.

It is commonplace, although true, to say that everything in our experience has two opposite faces: heat and cold, darkness and light, pleasure and pain, and that these are constantly exchanged. It is something that we verify in nature—the cold wind looks for the hot one to balance itself—something that was theorized as "compensation". Perhaps these are the most primary and primordial faces of the coin, but they are also for this very reason the most recognizable, to perceive life at all times. Everything in our world view has that double facet! We are always situated in front of one of the two faces, or aspects of perception, that we never look at simultaneously, but with which we identify alternately.

The so-called pendulum law is based on the idea that everything tries to meet its opposite, and move towards it—death follows life, sleep follows wakefulness, feeding after hunger. When we are in one place, we want to go to another! Such is always the case with pendular movements in our material and human condition, they have only two possible directions, to the right and to the left. The more force the pendulum has in this or that direction, with more energy does it return to the opposite. It is a vicious circle! Our whole existence goes from one point to another. Will it perhaps reach infinity to find harmony?

Shiva Nataraja embodies this universal paradox and transcends it at the same time. That is why he is, perhaps in his uniqueness, and in his surplus, the greatest inspirer of India as a culture and as a nation. He illuminates India in its extremes! He is the Lord of Death, but also of life and birth. Like the flames of fire, one of his symbols, the constant tension of change, flow, and transmutation vibrates in Shiva. He is the Lord of the transit between two states! He is the great transformer! The paradox is the language of the absolute, put in apparently incomprehensible and inexplicable terms. The genius of the paradox is based on its capacity for discovery of this brutal but effective imbalance of extremes. It tries to find a certain intuitive harmony, which is not simply textual, between opposites, and which on a higher plane enables it to find the way out of the maze.

If taken from their low point, literally from the bottom, paradoxes can be a cause of contradiction, chaos, accidents, or mishaps, since they are beyond all logic and order. At their opposite end, a surprising solution of meaning can be found, beyond the extremes, expressed by the will to search for a permanent balance, to go after peace and stability.

As highlighted in the Tantras, Shiva is the quintessential union of opposites, discipline (yoga) and enjoyment (*bhoga*). Among the ascetics he appears as the libertine, just as he is an ascetic among the libertines. He is a profound connoisseur of two types of fire, that of the ascetic and that of the lover. He is intimate with the scorching heat of ice, which extreme renunciation brings with it, and knows, equally, the cold that extreme sexual pleasure obtains. He knows how to take desire to its ultimate fulfilment, until it disappears by itself, and is sublimated with meditation. He obtains exaltation from both desire and asceticism, like ice that cools but also burns if put on skin for long. With Tapas, the spiritual fire, he defeats Kama, and pleasure is the reward. Pleasure on another plane. Exaltation on the threshold of Unity!

A long period of equilibrium gives rise to paralysis, and degeneration…hence the cyclic order of renewal and refreshment. It is about the difficult balance of drinking from the extremes and at the same time being in the middle point. Middle as balance in tension, as conquest of the best musical chord, never as mediocrity. Just like in a rope and rigging system with the sails of a boat, which instead of creating paralysis, facilitate gliding and speed. The entire cosmos seems to need that tension to exist!

Shiva is the Supreme Lord of the Underworld, Supreme Lord of the Nether World (Veerabhadra), but at the same time Lord of Brightness, Lord of Brilliance (Dhyutidhara), and Always Enlightened Ever-Radiant (Khanta). He is the Terrible (Rudra), as against the Compassionate (Dayalu). If it is true that in his destructive aspect, Shiva embodies Bhairava, the destroyer, it is also true that his great all encompassing role is fully represented by his form as Nataraja, who with his dance recreates the cosmos. Of course, these contradictions occur in mythological terms, since they are difficult or impossible to resolve on the human level. Yet we cannot help but live in the midst of the most diverse contradictions. There is no definitive state in existence!

Shiva manifests the pre-Aryan India, exemplified by Mohenjo Daro, and its advanced autochthonous civilization, while the first Vedic-Aryan gods, especially Rudra and Agni, who came from the West two millennia before Christ, are also present in him. He is the embodiment of lightning and fire! From Rudra he adopts one of his Vedic epithets, the Auspicious One, Shankar. Today those two worlds that converge and merge into him are difficult to distinguish—the Vedic and aristocratic elaborate ritual brought from distant lands, as against the native "primitive" one of elaborate animism. Shiva is the opposite of the ritualized figure of the main divinities of later Hinduism, such as Brahma (Creation), or Vishnu (Preservation), who are always themselves, static and immovable. In Shiva however there is a constant tension, a flow, so that everything that exists ends up sooner or later disappearing, cyclically transmuting itself into something else. He is the god of pure change! He inhabits the progression that tends to silence, to emptiness, and from there to fullness, to totality, encompassing the entire universe with the OM sound.

In the Mahabaratha, Shiva appears as one who has three eyes, who sees beyond time and the veil of dimensions. Referring to this dimension beyond the duality of time and space, many of the epithets that describe him have to do with the eyes, with the vision of the "God of the Three Eyes", or Tryambaka. Thus, he is the "Wide-eyed Lord" (Vishalaksha), "Lord of the Infinite Vision" (Anantadrishti), "Lotus-eyed Lord" (Kamalakshana), one with the Sun as Eye on the Forehead (Lalataksha), and he with the "Sun as the Eye" (Ravilochana). With his third eye he destroys desire, Kama, the Indian Cupid, who unsuccessfully tries to tempt him with all kinds of carnal delights, to divert him from his yogic concentration. Finally, however, the gods manage to persuade him to return desire to life, from the very ashes to which he had reduced it, and thus continue the movement and existence of everything in the world. Shiva finally accedes to their request. This is an unstoppable wheel that symbolizes the concentration and expansion of the cosmos! You have to accept change, and therefore death, as much as life. Shiva's vision penetrates beyond the illusion of maya. It transcends the matter/spirit disjunctive. He is everything and at the same time he is the non Being! He is the Void. Emptiness!

It seems that things happen in India as if someone had an accelerator hidden somewhere, and stepped on it, or stepped off it in an oscillating mode! In whatever situation! All or nothing! Up or down! There is no possibility of an intermediate point. What does all this remind me of? The repeated experience with my drivers always taking extreme action. It is striking that India recognizes itself only in these pendulum movements, in the successive union of the extremes. But perhaps, therein lies the peculiarity that nobody has managed to reveal! This happens, for example, in the depths of the caves of Ajanta and Ellora, dug in the 6th century in the centre of the country. From there, in an unpredictable leap of spirituality, coupled with eroticism, their Buddhist paintings come to mind that attest to the presence of one of the branches of the Silk Road. These paintings on the rocks of the caves excavated in the mountains, one of the most beautiful in this land, exhale a strange charm and majesty that permeates these subjugating and disturbing spaces. One would think that contrary assumptions cannot be linked! Desire and its extinction! Yes! Perhaps in this, especially in this, is the indefinable genius of India!

Starting with the Economy, public and private, everything in India is truly extreme, and as it entered the orbit of Capitalism in the 1990s, the market system and this way of life became more entrenched, supported as though by the Hindu conception of being favoured by the gods of fortune—Lakshmi and Ganesha. These gods help to overcome the difficulties of new projects and businesses, especially in the private sector. However, the echoes of the peculiar Socialism adopted in the first decades of Independence which continue to be heard in the country, fails to solve, or even tackle the great national problems. Is there a third or fourth way for India?

In the rejection of globalization, which has made the world smaller, more fluid and interconnected, but also riskier and more fragile, nationalisms and tribalisms of all kinds have been re-emerging in recent years. This is one of the blackest facets of these rapid world transformations. On this path, India is in clear danger of continuing an ultra-nationalist drift, as is being experienced in recent years. At the very least it implies a great risk of impoverishing its culture. India is already unique, it does not have to set out to be a world leader in anything material or commercial. But it finds itself in intense competition, even if not in a trade war, whether it wants to or not. It does not have to copy anyone, or achieve the ideals of others. It has its own! However it must try to put them to practice. It must move away from blind religious sectarianism. The identity of India is the opposite of the conflict of religions! There never has been until recently! Therefore, it should not fall into the error of its western neighbour Pakistan, since it goes against the country's very constitution, based on diversity. No nation should identify itself solely with a religious ideology, as in the case with Israel, as it inevitably means contempt for the rest of its inhabitants, if not their persecution.

The great challenge of this beloved country is to achieve a certain balance between tradition and the 21st century, to live in its great historical wealth, and at the same time help the majority of its citizens to achieve a dignified and evolved existence. However, as seen throughout the planet, such harmony between cultural legacy and modernity is hard to find, especially in large cities. It is in these cities that such a happy merger could best occur, due to the concurrence of historical places, museums and information, but it is precisely in big cities that it is more difficult to achieve due to the avalanche of migrants and limited space to solve the multitudinous problems that habitability entails. In a happy equalization between latest technology and respect for Earth, it would be desirable to find a balance between the huge ultra-modern buildings seen in major Indian cities, such as Mumbai, New Delhi or Bangalore, and Nature and its peaceful sanctuaries. Is it possible? Naturally yes, but at another stage of development, closer to that enjoyed by Singapore or Japan, with great national wealth, as well as great per capita well-being. Although none of these examples do anywhere near 1.3 billion people live!

In addition to achieving this comfortable economic situation, the most important thing is to clarify the borders and common points between the time of myth and modernity, allowing a flow between both, knowing how to take the best of each one, in a way that creates a cycle that feeds itself back. This means neither an irrational continuity of tradition, nor a surrender to new fashions, and becoming an absurd copy of them. Fortunately, today we still enjoy in India a mixed life system, which allows, for example, being shrewd in business, at the same time consulting astrologers! These two worlds are not seen as exclusive practices! Allowing imaginative swimming between hidden and manifest forces, the conscious and unconscious, on a collective scale.

It is the cultural actors, the university students, and the most affluent and educated society itself, who have a great role to play in uniting both extremes, which are the two engines of the social process, knowing how to move, in a matter of a few generations, from a purely traditional phase to an industrial and currently, a post-industrial one.

The reality is that the historical, hidden and intimate India, that spiritual accumulation of roots as inscrutable as deeply human and religious, has been gradually disappearing from the big cities. Thus, at least two worlds are being created—what it was, the venerated garden of the past, and what it wants to be, the commitment to an almost sci-fi future, although such a future may not finally fructify, due to the unavoidable weight of the disadvantaged two-thirds of the population. But India today, the famous emerging country, the emerged country… Where is it? Where do we find it? As in so many other emblematic sites, such as Venice for example, the most admired enclaves of this nation, in New Delhi or anywhere else, its palaces, forts, gardens, and natural sites, are in serious danger of becoming a "theme park", a distraction, reducing its identity to a framework of names—yoga, spirituality, religions, temples, ancient monuments and others. Yes, an image as evocative as India is, owing to past splendour in the world of art and spirit, today suggests, rather than a real and present space, a mental landscape of memory, and of longing, corresponding to that still image, seasoned with incense and curry, which we Westerners have. This is a matter of heated debate in certain forums, and there are many questions and interpretations about it. All of them can be summed up in this one question: Is Indian spirituality real or is it a myth belonging to the past?

One of the current trends which goes in this direction of future misunderstood, and which is a mistake, is to create satellite cities like Gurgaon or Noida in New Delhi, or Salt Lake City in Calcutta, places without soul, and exhausting because of the time it takes to reach them, due to the huge distance from the parent city. It is evident that solutions must be found for the pressing problem of overcrowding in these cities, but it is a serious failure to try to concentrate business and commercial activity in these "satellites", if the historical zones are not restored and improved before that. It is true that these historical spaces, like Old Delhi or Chandni Chowk, for example, are more and more dilapidated in all the traditional cities, sunk in excessive traffic, in chaos and dirt, but it is also true that they are frequented and inhabited by the bulk of their populations, and the true spirit of the city is found in them, the one that gives these cities their meaning and their vital breath. You cannot create uprooted satellites at the cost of neglecting and emptying what already exists! The dream would be to decongest and recover the traditional cities first, and on their outskirts, create well-connected smart cities, yes, as happily happens with the Electronic City, in the suburbs of Bangalore, known as the Silicon Valley of India.

Japan is a good example of a country without great natural resources, but which has gained great regional and global prominence since the middle of the 20th century. It has known how to design and represent the role of an undeniable leader in the entire Far-East, becoming a model for its neighbours, the so-called Asian Tigers, especially South Korea and Singapore, considered emerging economies until recently. Rooted in a vigorous culture and history, Japan belatedly and reluctantly followed the Western example, coming to parallel it, though arguably bettering it, in management, design, and technology. For example, it optimized the optics of the German cameras, knew how to equalize, or even improve cars and electronic devices, while keeping, albeit somewhat symbolically, its contact with the past. This has been idealized to a certain extent, and it acquires more and more the nuances of papier mâche, despite its undoubted beauty. It is true that in the palpable reality, not in the virtual one, there are those idyllic images of cherry blossoms that are seen in the photographs, the mountains with the temples in the forest, along with the many islands far from the hustle and bustle of big cities. But that is not all! There is also a lot of loneliness and lack of communication, and a rampant suicide cutting across all age groups, including children, as much as this peculiar way of ending one's life is rooted in the history of the country.

One of the conclusions, then, is that it is very difficult to master the counterpoint between the past and the future, between a brilliant and profound ancient culture, and extravagant development which does not ultimately lead to some type of imbalance. Many synonyms come to mind regarding this ideal of conjunction: harmony, counterweight, symmetry, stabilization and others. But they have not succeeded in Japan either! Torn between their past and their future, they neglected the present. They don't know how to live and enjoy life!

To modernize itself, more comprehensively, India does not need to look for external models. In its own culture, it has numerous elements, tools, and symbols that can inspire and build the different scenarios of the future. As always, however, it must know how to reinterpret and adapt all these possibilities to present circumstances. Otherwise, the much desired modernity will take many things ahead, destroying them, and arriving at an already irreparable situation of memory loss. What it urgently needs is an agile and free management. Yes, India must find its own formula for the future. Perhaps this is already written in the inscrutable plans of Mother India! And you just have to know how to listen to her! This nation can be a beacon to the world, or it can let the light that illuminated Rama on his way back, flicker out. Hopefully not!

Yoga, considered one of the exotic and traditional practices from India, has finally entered the West! This is a breakthrough for much of humanity. It has become acceptable in many parts of the world, slowly but forcefully especially because although it is an ancient technique it does not carry an ideology of any kind! Specialists in the world of wellness and self-help recommend, to this conglomerate of healthy life that has become a veritable industry, the practice of yoga and meditation. It is not without reason that yoga has become so universal, since it has numerous benefits for mental and somatic health. As a confirmation of this reality, in 2014, on an Indian initiative, the International Day of Yoga was created on June 21, coinciding with the summer solstice. This is undoubtedly a good symptom, this awareness on a global scale that the meaning of existence must be beyond instinct, pure survival, and the routine grind of work.

There are many centres across the globe where weekend intensive courses are held and several schools where yoga is taught. In them the emphasis is placed on breathing and relaxation, on postures, and finally on meditation. The benefits for the body are exalted, it improves energy levels, enhances the feeling of well-being, by moderately massaging the internal organs, and helps achieve a certain mental serenity in the face of the small or large dramas of daily life. In short, yoga contributes to achieving a development for the body and mind in a sustainable way.

According to legend, Patanjali who is said to have established this timeless practice for mental, bodily and spiritual health, learnt it while still in the womb of his mother, Gonika, where Shiva himself incarnated through two avatars.

The Yoga Sutras of Patanjali, composed in the 3rd century BC, the most pragmatic as well as illuminating spiritual study of all times, are perhaps a unique achievement of human civilization. These 195 aphorisms (sutras), or short phrases made up of very specific terminology and grammar, work surprisingly well for the mind and body of any human being of any time.

Yoga has eight well-differentiated branches within its unified field. Three of them are purely physical, while the rest concern ethics, the world of spirituality and meditation. In turn, yoga is one of the six philosophies or doctrines (*darsana*) of Hinduism. The first of these eight yogic branches, Yama, belongs to ethical life, involves non-violence, not harming any living being, as well as avoiding carnal pleasure and other excesses, thus intensifying detachment from material objects. Next, Niyama touches on self-discipline, healthy living, and rigorous hygiene, which leads to increasing one's powers through austerity and concentration, as well as cultivating the inner breath that tends towards the divine. One step further, the third branch, the Asana, deals with the organism's disposition for meditation, that is, body positions and their direct psychosomatic effects. Pranayama, or conscious control of breathing, maintains the body's energy regulation through inhalation/expiration rhythms, as well as prevents distraction of the mind. The fifth branch of this spiritual technique is the Pratyahara, which deals with recollection in oneself, avoiding the environment and the senses that govern us, in an action/reaction dynamic. Dharana tends to the concentration of the mind, with or without the help of elements such as the yantra, or the mandala, to fix attention without effort. The penultimate section of yoga, Dhyana, seeks to stimulate the state of objectless meditation, that is, non-reflection. It has nothing to do with thoughts, but rather the contrary, with observing such thoughts as something alien, as "passing clouds", in order to calmly move away from them. Samadhi is the last scale of yoga, in which both the mind and the body stop disturbing the horizon of consciousness, and consciousness tends in its purest state to union with the non-personalized divinity.

The practice of yoga strengthens the connections of neurons, synapses, yielding unusual findings. It sharpens perception, contributes to overcoming the tired internal dialogue, which only reinforces, and torments the ego, reduces stress and anxiety, improves mental health, and therefore the quality of life. Indeed, according to already available objective data from the studies that have been carried out, it contributes to eradicating or reducing many of the diseases linked to stress and anxiety. Insofar as it deactivates the strategies of the dominating ego, it undoubtedly helps, in the medium and long term, to improve interpersonal relationships. This is all very good! But yoga is much more than that! And therefore the real danger is that it stops only here!

A degree or step beyond "physical" yoga is meditation, which is nothing but connecting with the root of one's own being, with the true self. We need to get out of the instrument of the mind itself, place ourselves on the other side of the intellect, to see it from the outside, to observe it from another perspective, and not necessarily identify with it. Meditation is a place beyond the action, because it happens as in an "awake dream". In effect, meditation is a going beyond the habituated resources, navigating beyond the mind, beyond its goals or strategies, even beyond yoga in the technical sense.

Meditation is the spontaneous and undirected putting into play of our deepest resources, it is reaching Unity after the illusion of separation. At that level, that of the spirit, we are all one. Although meditation is something practiced in the individual space it will have a global sweep shortly!

This is a fabulously unique system that works like a perfect machine. You do not have to believe in anything, it is not a matter of faith, religion or ideology. It is true that in the historical context in which it emerged, it is close to the Hindu and Buddhist conception of the world, although it operates in a basic way as a technique, as something simply practical, such as exercising, with the additional advantage of influencing the mind and the spirit.

Equally unique is the form in which the anonymous authors composed the most sacred Indian texts. *Shruti*, which in Samskrit means "what is heard", makes up the most sacred and primeval of religious literature in Hinduism, and is said to be transmitted by a divine and mysterious revelation to certain sages (rishi). Through the centuries, it has given texts such as the four Vedas, the Aranyakas, the Brahmanas (ritual treatises), and the Upanishads. Such revelation on the part of these fantastic yogis took place through direct experience (*anubhava*). The other type of transmission, which is not inspired, but "copied", is *Smriti*, "that which is remembered", and which also forms an important part of the Hindu textual chain, examples being the *Puranas*, among others. While *Shrutis* are very ancient, with very precise recitation techniques maintained through the centuries, *Smriti* is slightly older than our common era.

After the end of the British rule, an institutional secularism was promoted in India, parallel to a democratic process, quite lengthy and complex, in which the separation of powers prevailed. From this great clash of local and foreign cultural and social models that ended with Independence and Partition, at least something of the best in Europe remained for India—democracy, based on the aforementioned separation of powers. These elements constitute the necessary basis for the rule of law and the birth of a middle class, the avowed ideal of the common good, and they represent the most positive aspect of the long engagement with the British, in that rare and explosive mixture of admiration and hatred that marked their relationship of several centuries. The operation of justice, slow and irregular, but existent, is, despite high corruption, vital for the emergence and foundation of a solid civil society. In recent decades, there have been many changes in the country, such as the Prevention of Sati act of 1987, the progressive secularization of the caste system, a more active role for women, both in the positions they hold and in the decisions about their own life, marriage, access to education and more. But there is still much to be done!

Gandhi and Nehru symbolize two very different visions in their essence, although they were complementary in the time immediately prior to Independence. Represented with intensity by their personalities, they embody two very different Indias. One, the practical and "realistic" India of Nehru, who said that "dams are the temples of modern India", and the other, that of Gandhi, who sought to create a future in his ultra traditional way, a faithful mirror of the idealized past, that of the "religion of eternal India", Sanatana Dharma, without mechanized industry, without modern healthcare, without airports. But between these two temporal and conceptual extremes, India needs a present. A present through which a certain well-being can reach the many millions of disadvantaged. This latter vision of the country has been permanently stranded in a dry dock. The reason was none other than a "bath of realism", caused by the brutal competition between the world trade blocs, relocation of businesses, and other turmoil that the complex 21st century brought with it. As spiritual and deep as its roots are, in the face of these unavoidable presences, no nation can be left behind in the race, and less so when it has 1.3 billion people. This is a reality that must be faced in order to offer minimum opportunities for education, health, work, communications, and everything else that would help the country come out of the social paralysis in which much of India finds itself. Gandhi's actions must be placed in a specific context, which was that of Freedom from the British Empire. As is evident, they were not geared towards generating growth and stability of a country, of a subcontinent as a whole, a subcontinent that is facing the 21st century, but whose management structures remain largely stagnant in the past.

Nobody has been able to formulate what the true unifying element, the decisive one, was that preserved India in the most crucial moments of its formation as a nation, and defines it today as what it is—a unique people amidst this limitless mosaic of languages, races, and religions. It is no secret that there were many risks on that distant August 15, 1947, when India became truly independent for the first time in its long history, uniting all its princely states to end up taking shape in 29 units. The partition with Pakistan would seriously jeopardize the survival of an aspiration, an idea common to all the communities and religions that make up India.

In this complicated game of equilibrium that occurred at that time, with enormous risks for the country, among the most successful measures taken by the founders of the "new", yet such an old homeland, was undoubtedly the creation of a federal and democratic nation/State, with respect for all its immense human variety. Despite the very dark moments that it undeniably went through, and which culminated in its division into two different nations, seen today in perspective, the success of the integrity and continuity of the country is owed largely to the legacy of Gandhi. Faced with corruption and selfishness, he put forward compassion and equality among all. In this regard, he said that if you want to change the world, change yourself. That is to say, without inner peace, no form of peace can be achieved or transmitted.

Such a great change in practice, led by such a special figure, could not but have had unprecedented consequences. The peaceful revolution was like a beneficial boomerang, which then hit back, had its return, although sometimes it is forgotten. Gandhi invoked maximal ethics, which consists in setting an example oneself, declaring that life is a mirror that always returns what is done, which is close to the concept of karma. It is like saying, what I am, the world is. The message, the action and the model, in this way, were a single piece, a single coin. Gandhi, in fact, was one of those rare human beings who came close to complete transparency. He was sincere in his work and thus in his autobiography, recognizes his dark spots and his "failures" in a long difficult life. But the result was that his method of non-violent "active resistance" triumphed in India and outside.

Today, this country, like the entire planet, is in a process of globalization that affects many fields, such as communications, methods of industrial and agricultural development, trade, education, etc. India cannot betray itself in this process, confusing the means with the objectives. The goal is a decent life for most people, and the means, resources and policy to manage it The complex, and at the same time clear markers of historical identity of India are meditation, its spiritual way of life, the notion that all physical change is preceded and made possible by a spiritual and mental change, as Gandhi reminded us. He was not an economist! Surely today he would be overwhelmed explaining us the strategies of development in this complex world, as well as the most successful mechanisms of market regulation and redistribution of wealth. However, he is largely at the origin of that universal saying today, "Think global, act local." Faced with these facts, he harvested a great victory that broke through on its own. Gandhi was local in action, although universalist in his thinking. The Bhagavad Gita was his favourite book, but he took many ideas and reflections from Jainism, Buddhism and also Christianity, and writers like Tolstoy and Thoreau.

Globalization is the result of a long historical process that begins with the printing press and even before that, with the old maritime and land routes. Obviously, it involves many good things and many bad ones too, although the homogenisation of the entire globe, with the impoverishment of cultures, the disappearance of peculiarities and differences, the growing disparity between the rich, who are getting richer and the poor getting poorer, are some of its negative consequences.

India today has clearly opted for modernity, understood as progress, and that has no turning back. It is not possible to have a spinning wheel (a charkha) at home to make oneself clothes. The country has to grow in diverse industries and infrastructures. But what Gandhi warns us against is the absolute dominion and possession of the market. He proposes another more human model! That is not allowing oneself to be obsessed by the need for consumption, beyond what is logically necessary and warns against the thirst to possess, consumption for consumption's sake. He speaks to us about the need for authenticity as against appearances, and the need for all to lead a dignified life in a country of such abysmal differences. Virtually, all principles advocated by Gandhi are not only valid but necessary in this era of globalization. Today, so often we know more of something that has happened thousands of miles away but not what happens in front of our door. The principle of non-violence, ahimsa, continues to be relevant and applicable. In fact, it is the foundation of a sustainable future for humanity and the Earth. "There are no roads for peace, peace is the only road." It is evident that Gandhi's doctrine of non-violence, which has not always been followed, did not succeed, because twenty-five years after his death India became a nuclear power. But then it is equally true that there were, and are, many territorial and other threats.

Seventy years after the assassination of Gandhi, it can be said that his legacy for the 21st century is his own example, in the emphasis placed on the "being", not possessing, and on the universal values of the human being. The most important aspect of that legacy is to ensure the dignity of each and every one of its people, going beyond power relations, imposed earlier by the colonial power, and today, by the market forces and their ideology of consumerism.

Much more than the Indus, which gives the country its short and majestic name, the Ganges referred to with respect by the Hindus as *Maa Ganga*, Mother Ganges, is not only a river in India. It is not even just the first of the national rivers, but it constitutes THE RIVER par excellence, as the Taj Mahal is among the monuments, Everest among the mountains, or Goa among the beaches. With a rich mythology accumulated over the centuries, the Ganges is indeed looked upon as a mother, as well as a goddess, Ganga Devi, sent by Brahma, the great Creator, to purify the ashes of the dead. According to tradition, the god of creative destruction, Shiva, also took part in its birth, causing its waters, which mercilessly flooded the earth from the sky, to fall on to his own head, then sliding down his long ascetic mane, and making the river return to its course, thus bringing, once again well-being and fertility to its inhabitants.

Also for this reason, it is the most important of the seven sacred rivers of Hinduism, with the high point of its journey in the city of

Benares, the ancient Kashi of infinite legends, where thousands of people from the three old religions that were born here (Hinduism, Buddhism and Jainism) bathe every morning with the sunrise to purify themselves internally and externally.

Ablution in the very first hours is the most important moment of the day for such practitioners on this historic waterway. It does not matter that this constitutes an absolute paradox in itself, as in its entire journey, the Ganges is most polluted at Benares! After its cold and clean waters have descended from the western summits of the Himalayas, in distant Gangotri, they reach their mouth next to Calcutta, turned into infected mud. As is known, the discharges of the sewers flow into it, as well as effluents from the industries, the small shipyards and tanneries, along with many other highly toxic elements.

As much as such water is drunk and revered as an other-wordly and magically purifying element, the reality is that more than a million coliform bacteria from human waste are present per 100 millilitres. To calibrate this data, it must be taken into account that according to the World Health Organization, bathing begins to be dangerous when there are more than 500 bacteria in suspension in this quantity of water. It exceeds this by 2,000 times. Two thousand times! The result is that until its mouth, where it is already connected to the Brahmaputra, in the Sundarbans mangroves, declared by UNESCO in 1997 a World Heritage Site, there are several places in a terminal state. From agriculture to small and large industries, its waters provide sustenance for thousands or millions of families, and create one of the most varied ecosystems in the world, but there seems to be little concern about it.

There is a governmental Action Plan for the Ganges, but it is an open secret that up to now it has been a great failure due to the country's habitual resistance to any progress, summarized in corruption and bureaucracy, and additionally in this case, the lack of appropriate technology to confront the great challenge. In 2018 it was declared the "leader" among the ten most polluted rivers in the world, by the Helmholtz Centre dedicated to environmental research, since it adds more than half a million tons of plastic waste per year to marine pollution.

Respect for the Ganges is part of the Indian identity, its culture and civilization over the centuries. It is known as the River of Life and along its approximately 3000 km route it nurtures and nourishes millions of forms of life. And yet today the Ganges is a great dying being that runs the risk of becoming the opposite of what it was from time immemorial.

Hopefully this does not become a metaphor for India in this destructive dynamic, succumbing to industrial growth and overpopulation!

May the creative face of Kali dominate over her own other face, that of the destroyer, and this unique river escape the risk of remaining great only in name.